SHERLOCK

HOLMES

THE SIGN OF

FOUR

By Sir Arthur Conan Doyle
Adapted by Nick Lane

Published by Playdead Press 2018

© Nick Lane 2018

Nick Lane has asserted his rights under the Copyright, Design and Patents Act, 1988, to be identified as the authors of this work.

A CIP catalogue record for this book is available from the British Library.

ISBN 978-1-910067-69-7

Playdead Press
www.playdeadpress.com

Sherlock Holmes: The Sign of Four

By Sir Arthur Conan Doyle
Adapted by Nick Lane

**Produced by Blackeyed Theatre
in association with New Theatre Royal Portsmouth and South
Hill Park Arts Centre**

Cast

Sherlock Holmes	**Luke Barton**
Dr John Watson	**Joseph Derrington**
Mary Morstan / Mrs Hudson	**Stephanie Rutherford**
Thaddeus Sholto / Major Sholto	**Ru Hamilton**
Dost Akbar / Athelney-Jones	**Christopher Glover**
Jonathan Small / Captain Morstan	**Zach Lee**

All other parts played by members of the cast

Artistic Team

Writer & Director	**Nick Lane**
Composer	**Tristan Parkes**
Set Designer	**Victoria Spearing**
Lighting Designer	**Claire Childs**
Costume Designer	**Naomi Gibbs**
Movement Director	**Emma Webb**
Company Stage Manager	**Caroline Sheard**
Press Relations	**Chloe Nelkin Consulting**
Education Advisors	**Danielle Corbishley**
	Liz Allum
Set Construction	**Russell Pearn**
	Steve Spearing
Scenic Art	**Jane O'Sullivan**
	Sophie Spearing
Production Assistant	**Kirsty McDougall**
Producer	**Adrian McDougall**

Blackeyed Theatre would like to thank to Scott Ramsay, Craig Titley, the staff of New Theatre Royal Portsmouth and South Hill Park Arts Centre, Arts Council England

Luke Barton | *Sherlock Holmes*

Luke trained at the Oxford School of Drama.

His recent credits include: *The Unexpected Guest, Spider's Web* (The Mill at Sonning, directed by Brian Blessed), *Twelfth Night, Romeo & Juliet, A Midsummer Night's Dream* and *Henry V* (UK Tour for Merely Theatre), *Reunion, Echoes, Absent* and *After Three Sisters* for Living Record Productions (Edinburgh Festivals / Brockley Jack Theatre), *Misterman* and *L'Etranger* (Liverpool Everyman and Playhouse).

Joseph Derrington | *Dr John Watson*

Joseph graduated from The School of The Arts (University of Northampton) in 2014. He has since worked with directors Laurie Sansom, James Farrell (RSC Associate Director) and Jamie Rocha Allan (Frantic Assembly and Associate Director, RSC).

Theatre credits include: *The Canterville Ghost* (Erasmus Theatre touring Italy), *Stinksville* (Arletty Theatre: UK Tour), *The Importance Of Being Earnest* (Bruiser Theatre at MAC Theatre Belfast), *Tyke* (Arts Theatre / Edinburgh Fringe), *The Lost Carnival: The Battle Of The Carnivals* (LAS Theatre / Wild Rumpus Theatre), *The Dumb Waiter* (Maltings Arts Theatre), *The Bacchae* (Royal & Derngate) and *The Crucible* (Looking Glass Theatre).

Screen credits include: *Birdsong* (Working Title) and *William And Mary* (Granada Television).

Christopher Glover | *Dost Akbar, Adnan, Chowdar, Athelney-Jones, Khan*

Christopher has performed extensively in the UK, Ireland and Australia, and he was an original member of Irish theatre company, *Tinderbox*. Theatre includes: *Aladdin* and *Alice in Wonderland* (16feet), *Peckham The Soap Opera*, *Who Cares* (Royal Court) and *5 Steps* (Royal Court Tottenham).

His film & TV credits include: *Eastenders* (BBC), *Touching Evil* (ITV), *Rules of Engagement* (ITV), Dennis Potter's *Karaoke* (BBC / Channel 4), *The Bill* (ITV), *Underworld* (Hat Trick / Channel 4), *Hollyoaks* (Lime Pictures / Channel 4) and *Casualty* (BBC). He was in the 2014 film *Heard* and in 2017 *America's War On Drugs* (Talos Films) as Mexican Drug Lord "El Chapo".

In Australia, his theatre credits include: *Constance Drinkwater* (Darwin Festival / Tour), *7 Deadly Australian Sins* and *Gods of Spicy Things* (Australian Tours). He also played three characters simultaneously in Scott Witt's comedy *Macbeth*. As Associate Director of Jute Theatre Australia, he directed the original productions of *Cake* (Tropic Sun / JUTE Tour), *The Shining Path* (Queensland Tour) and *Dancing Back Home* (Mudlark Tasmania), while his play *The Mad Mile* was nominated for several awards.

Ru Hamilton | *Thaddeus Sholto, Major Sholto, Sherman, Thomas*

Trained at Rose Bruford College. Ru is an actor, musician, composer and musical director.

He plays the cello, clarinet, flute, saxophone, piano, double bass and ukulele.

Theatre credits include: *Treasure Island* (Birmingham Rep), *Tipping The Velvet* (Lyric Hammersmith), *Peter Pan* (Derby

Theatre), *Farm Boy* (Mercury, Colchester), *Roundelay* (Southwark Playhouse), *Titus Andronicus* (Smooth Faced Gentlemen), *Fragment R&D* (Iron Shoes) and *Rise* (Old Vic New Voices).

Zach Lee | *Jonathan Small, Captain Morstan, McMurdo, Matthews*

Zach trained at The Arts Educational School a long time ago!

Recent work in theatre includes: *The Strange Case of Dr Jekyll & Mr Hyde* (Blackeyed Theatre UK tour) *Bouncers, A Weekend In England, Glass Menagerie, Dr Faustus, Frankenstein, Wuthering Heights, Little Malcolm And His Struggle Against The Eunochs, A Christmas Carol, Unleashed* and *Reunion,* for which he received a nomination for Best Actor at the 2003 Manchester Evening News Awards (all Hull Truck), *The Derby McQueen Affair* (York Theatre Royal), *Round The Twist* (Eastern Angles), *The Winters Tale* (Nulty / Pilton Productions), *Treasure Island* (Harrogate Theatre), *South* (Shred Productions), *Five Kinds of Silence* (Stepping Out Theatre), *The Wife* (Rude Mechanicals), *Romeo & Juliet, 100, Some Voices* (Alchemy Theatre Co), *Moby Dick* and *Frankenstein: Revelations* (Theatre Mill) and *Monopoleyes* (Stolen Thread). He has written & produced two plays, *Geoffrey Ramsbottom – Man of the 90s* (Tabard Theatre) and *Two Brothers And One World Cup* (Underbelly, Edinburgh Festival / UK Tour).

His television credits include: *Emmerdale, Coronation Street, Crime Traveller, Class Act* (ITV), *Young Dracula* (CBBC), *In The Club* (BBC), *The Contract, Sickness And Health, Feelgood Factor* (Channel 4), Lynda La Plante's *The Governor* (ITV) and *Underbelly* (CH 9 Australia).

Films include: *Chasing Dreams, Hard Edge* (DMS Films), *Mortal Fools* (Virtual World Productions) and *The Creature Below* (Dark Rift Films).

Stephanie Rutherford | *Mary Morstan, Mrs Hudson, Mrs Smith, Joanna*

Stephanie trained at Rose Bruford in Actor-Musicianship, graduating in 2015 with first class honours.

Theatre credits include *Kubla Khan, Mirror Mirror,* King Leontes / Mariner / Sheep in *In a Pickle* (Oily Cart. Both UK / USA Tour), *The Frugal Horn, Now That's What I Call Music* (Presence Theatre), *Pulse* (Bamboozle), *Down To Earth* (Bamboozle @ Imaginate Festival), *Hansel and Gretel* (Bamboozle @ Leicester Curve), Sister / Teeth the Rat in *Cinderella* (Derby Theatre) and *My Filthy Hunt* (Holden Street Theatres, Adelaide Fringe).

Nick Lane | Adapter & Director

Nick's Stage adaptations include *The Strange Case of Dr. Jekyll & Mr Hyde* (Blackeyed Theatre in 2017 and previously Hull Truck and Theatre Mill), *The Wakefield Mysteries* (Theatre Royal Wakefield), *Frankenstein, Lady Chatterley's Lover* (Hull Truck) and *1984* (Northern Broadsides), as well as a co-adaptation of *Moby Dick* for Hull Truck with his friend John Godber. Original adult plays include: *The Derby McQueen Affair* (York Theatre Royal), *My Favourite Summer, Blue Cross Xmas, Me & Me Dad* (Hull Truck), *Housebound, Seconds Out* (Reform), *Hopeless Romantics* (Reform, co-written with Fiona Wass), *Royal Flush* and *Odd Job Men* (Rich Seam Theatre). His play *The Goal* receives its premiere at the Courtyard, Hereford, in October 2018.

Nick is also an accomplished children's playwright, and his credits include *A Christmas Carol, Beauty & The Beast, The Hunchback of Notre Dame* and *The Snow Queen* (Hull Truck), *Pinocchio, A Scarborough Christmas Carol* (Stephen Joseph Theatre), *Snow White* and *Little Red Riding Hood* (York Theatre Royal), *The Elves & The Shoemaker* (Courtyard, Hereford) and *Hansel & Gretel* (Pilot). His original work for children includes the acclaimed *Ginger Jones and the Sultan's Eye* (Polka / Drum Theatre Plymouth / York Theatre Royal), *'Twas The Night Before Christmas, When Santa Got Stuck in the Fridge* and *A Christmas Fairytale* (Hull Truck). For Christmas 2018, Nick has adapted *Alice In Wonderland* for the Stephen Joseph Theatre and a new version of *Snow White* for the Courtyard, Hereford.

As well as directing the majority of his own work, Nick's directing credits include *The Glass Menagerie, Departures, Life's A Beach, Studs, Beef, Amateur Girl, Lucky Sods* and *Ring Around the Humber* (Hull Truck), *April in Paris, Two, September in the Rain* and *Little Italy* (York Theatre Royal).

Tristan Parkes | Composer

Tristan has composed, designed sound and musically directed material for film, theatre, major events and television for over a decade. This includes over fifteen productions for Hull Truck Theatre, multiple productions for the Edinburgh Festival including *An Audience with Jimmy Saville* staring Alistair McGowan 2015, over a decade of productions for The National Youth Theatre of Great Britain, most recently Tatty Hennessy's play *F-OFF* (Criterion) and their 60th Anniversary Gala at the Shaftsbury Theatre in the West End. Tristan was a musical director on the Beijing and London Olympic Games and a composer for the British Pavilion at the World Expo' in Shanghai. Film work includes *To All the Girls I've Loved Before* (Channel 4 Films), *When Romeo Met Juliet* (BBC) and *Anna Karenina* (Working Title Films).

Most recent theatre work includes *Deeds Not Words*, a musical theatre piece in memory of murdered MP Jo Cox and performed by The Batley and Spen Youth Theatre Company set up in her honour. *Sherlock Holmes: The Sign of Four* and *The Strange Case of Dr Jekyll & Mr Hyde* (Blackeyed Theatre), a national tour of *Dead Sheep* by Johnathan Maitland, *Goat Song* for London Contemporary Dance, *Frankenstein Revelations* (York Theatre Royal) and *#Hashtag Lightie* (Arcola Theatre). Tristan has just completed adapting famed children's author Julian Donaldson's book *Tabby McTat* into a musical which tours nationally from September 2018.

Tristan is an Education Associate for the Donmar Warehouse and Lyric Hammersmith theatres and regularly facilitates music and theatre workshops across the country. He is Programme Leader for Performing Arts at the University of East London.

Victoria Spearing | Designer

Graduating from Bretton Hall in Theatre Design and Technology in 2001, Victoria started work as a freelance set designer with South Hill Park Arts Centre, where she is now resident designer.

This will be the twenty-first design for Blackeyed Theatre, from *The Caretaker* to the highly acclaimed tours of *Not About Heroes, Dracula* and *Teechers*. Her design for *The Beekeeper* was nominated for the Best Set Design in the 2012 Off West End Theatre Awards.

She has designed over one hundred sets for a variety of companies, producing initial sketches and model boxes through to involvement in set building, painting and final dressing.

For South Hill Park she has designed the last twelve pantomimes, as well as a range of in-house productions, including *Summer Holiday, Brassed Off, Stepping Out, Blood Brothers, Calendar Girls, Oliver, Henry V, The Tempest, Billy Elliot* and *Oh What A Lovely War*. She also redesigned South Hill Park's Wilde Theatre Bar and Foyer to create a new performance space.

Her design work for other companies includes the world premiere of *A Little History of the World* (Watermill Theatre), *The Dumb Waiter, Miss Julie, Waiting for Godot, Race* and *The Nativity that Goes Wrong* (Reading Rep), *Journey's End, Dancing at Lughnasa, The Madness of George III, Three Men in a Boat* and *Birdsong* (Original Theatre Company), *Lotty's War* (Giddy Ox), *Loserville* (Youth Music Theatre), *The History Boys* and *Danny the Champion of the World* (London Contemporary Theatre), as well as various Christmas shows for The Castle Wellingborough.

Naomi Gibbs | Costume Designer

Naomi is resident costume designer at New Theatre Royal Portsmouth having become an associate artist in 2016 and enjoyed regular projects there since 2010. This is her third project with

Blackeyed Theatre as costume designer, following *The Strange Case of Doctor Jekyll and Mr Hyde* (2017) and *Teechers* (2018).

Naomi has had a varied costuming career in theatre, events and the music industry, and she has recently designed for Stopgap Dance Company, Blackeyed Theatre, New Theatre Royal and Adam Ant. She also undertakes private commissions to design and make costumes and bespoke pieces. For the second year running, she will use her vintage fashion knowledge to head wardrobe backstage at The Goodwood Revival Fashion Emporium with fashion events company, Fashion Live.

Current work in production includes *Peter Pan* at The New Theatre Royal (Christmas 2018) and four new productions (as yet unannounced) for 2019.

Examples of her work can be found at www.societybelle.co.uk

Claire Childs | Lighting Designer

Claire studied Mathematics at Lady Margaret Hall, Oxford before going into the theatre as a lighting designer and technician.

Claire has previously worked with Blackeyed Theatre as Lighting Designer on *The Strange Case of Dr Jekyll & Mr Hyde*, Company Stage Manager for tours of *The Trial* and *Not About Heroes* and as Re-lighter for *The Great Gatsby*.

Her lighting design credits include UK tours of *I Am Beast, Killing Roger* and *The Girl with No Heart* for Sparkle and Dark, *The Tempest* (Thick as Thieves), *The Shipwrecked House* (Penned in the Margins) and *The Just So Stories* (Red Table Theatre). Other lighting designs include *Mozart vs Machine* at Folkestone Quarterhouse, *Magnyfycence* at Hampton Court Palace, *The Barrier* (Park Theatre), *1000 Songs* (Arcola Theatre), *Venus/Mars* (Old Red Lion Theatre / Bush Theatre), *Picasso is Coming... Ce Soir* (St James Theatre) and *A Midsummer Night's Dream* (Glamis Adventure Playground).

Lighting designs for dance productions include the UK tours of *NowHere* (Divya Kasturi), *Dracula – Welcome to D's* (Chantry Dance Company), and *Forgot Your Password?* (The Purcell Room, Southbank Centre).

www.clairechilds.co.uk

Emma Webb | Movement Director

Emma Webb trained as a movement director at Royal central School of Speech and Drama. She has recently worked with South Hill Park, Oxford Playhouse, Human Story Theatre, Red Dog Theatre Company and Justice in Motion among others.

Caroline Sheard | Company Stage Manager

Caroline trained at East 15 Acting School on the Stage Management and Technical Theatre course. She has worked in a vast range of venues, including Theatr Clwyd on *The Importance of Being Earnest* and The Point in Eastleigh on *Little Red Riding Hood*. Caroline has been involved in various tours throughout her career, including *Odd Job Men* (Rich Seam) and *Across the Dark Water* (The Berry Theatre, Hedge End), as well as many site-specific adventures around the country, including *Frankenstein Revelations* by Nick Lane (theatre Mill). She frequently takes part in the Edinburgh Fringe Festival as a Venue Manager with theSpaceUK, in their largest venue, Surgeons Hall.

Adrian McDougall | Producer

Adrian is the founder and Artistic Director of Blackeyed Theatre. He grew up in Berkshire, studying modern languages at Southampton University, going on to work in marketing and PR, before becoming a theatre producer in 2004.

Since Blackeyed Theatre's very first production, *Effie's Burning*, he has produced twenty-four national tours, including the world premiere of Steven Berkoff's *Oedipus* and brand new stage adaptations of Bram Stoker's *Dracula,* F. Scott Fitzgerald's *The Great Gatsby* and Mary Shelley's *Frankenstein*. As a director, his credits include – for Blackeyed Theatre – the world premiere of *The Beekeeper* and national tours of *Oh What A Lovely War*, *Teechers* and *Alfie*, as well as *Brassed Off* and *House And Garden* (for South Hill Park). He has also worked as an actor, touring the UK with Oddsocks Productions, Premiere Stage Productions and the Phoenix Theatre Company.

Adrian is also a director of CentreStage Partnership, a leading provider of experiential learning and behavioural coaching to organisations from the public and private sectors; www.cstage.co.uk.

He lives in Bracknell with his wife and two young children, supporting and participating in community theatre when he has time!

Chloé Nelkin Consulting | Press Relations

Chloé Nelkin Consulting was founded in 2010 and specialises in PR, events, marketing and consultancy with a dedicated focus on visual and performing arts. With a passion for the arts and communicating the importance of culture to today's society, CNC is a dynamic company that always delivers with style and sophistication. The company handles multiple sell-out productions of all sizes across all genres of theatre. Some recent theatre work includes: *Dust* (Soho Theatre / Edinburgh), *A Gym Thing* (Pleasance Theatre), *Devil with the Blue Dress* (Bunker Theatre), *Plastic* (Old Red Lion), CircusFest 2018 (Roundhouse), *Inside Pussy Riot* (Saatchi Gallery), *The Red Lion* (Trafalgar Studios), *An Inspector Calls* (Playhouse Theatre), *Land of Our Fathers* (English Tour / Found111), *My Mother Said I Never Should* (St. James Theatre), *BU21* (Theatre503 / Trafalgar Studios), Sasha Regan's all-male *HMS Pinafore* (UK Tour) and *Brodsky/Baryshnikov* (Apollo Theatre).

www.chloenelkinconsulting.com.

BLACKEYED
THEATRE

Blackeyed Theatre has been creating exciting, sustainable theatre throughout the UK since 2004. We have taken our work to over a hundred different theatres across England, Scotland and Wales, from 50 seat studios to 1000 seat opera houses.

Central to everything we do is our desire both to challenge and engage artists and audiences. As a company that receives minimal funding, we are proof that commercially successful theatre can still be innovative and can still surprise. We believe that only by balancing a desire to push artistic boundaries with an appreciation of what audiences have a desire to see do you create theatre that is truly sustainable, both commercially and artistically. We bring together artists with a genuine passion for the work they produce, offering a theatrical experience that's both artistically excellent, affordable and accessible.

Our previous national tours include *The Strange Case of Dr Jekyll And Mr Hyde* (Robert Louis Stevenson, adapted by Nick Lane), *Frankenstein* (Mary Shelley, adapted by John Ginman), *The Great Gatsby* (F. Scott Fitzgerald, adapted by Stephen Sharkey), *Not About Heroes* (Stephen MacDonald), *Dracula* (Bram Stoker, adapted by John Ginman), *Teechers* (John Godber), *Mother Courage And Her Children* (Bertolt Brecht), *The Trial* (Steven Berkoff), *The Caucasian Chalk Circle* (Bertolt Brecht), *Alfie* (Bill Naughton), *The Cherry Orchard* (Anton Chekhov), *Oh What a Lovely War* (Joan Littlewood), the world premiere of *Oedipus* (Steven Berkoff) and *The Resistible Rise of Arturo Ui* (Bertolt Brecht). In 2011, Blackeyed Theatre launched Pulse, a new-writing competition. The winning script, *The Beekeeper*, enjoyed a three-week London Fringe run, receiving three OFFIE nominations, including Best New Play.

The company is resident at South Hill Park Arts Centre in Bracknell, where we continue to create accessible theatre that challenges expectations, furthering our reputation as one of the UK's leading touring theatre companies.

"One of the most innovative, audacious companies working in contemporary English theatre"
The Stage

www.blackeyedtheatre.co.uk | @blackeyedtheatr

NEW THEATRE ROYAL

Established as a theatre in 1856, New Theatre Royal has enjoyed over 160 years as a cultural landmark in the heart of Portsmouth. The theatre re-opened in October 2015 after undergoing a £4.5m refurbishment project to restore the historic building back to its former glory and bring it into the 21st century.

New Theatre Royal, Portsmouth was awarded one of the largest uplifts in National Portfolio Organisation funding from Arts Council England (ACE) for the April 2018 to March 2022 period, allowing it to further develop its work and focus on four key areas – the programme of work on-stage, artist development, digital development and internationalism.

The theatre delivers an eclectic programme of diverse acts and events, including theatrical classics, comedy shows and musical performances, as well as facilitating and inspiring creative talent in the locality.

Committed to making theatre more accessible to audiences, New Theatre Royal recently introduced a Pay What You Can scheme on a few selected performances as well as offering £10 tickets for those aged 16 to 25.

www.newtheatreroyal.com

The New Theatre Royal Trustees (Portsmouth) Limited
Registered Charity No: 271976

New Theatre Royal
20 – 24 Guildhall Walk
Portsmouth
Hampshire
PO1 2DD

South Hill Park Arts Centre has been at the creative heart of Berkshire for over 40 years. This picturesque 18th century mansion house in Bracknell houses two theatres, a dance studio, visual arts spaces, artists in residence, a comedy club, resident associate companies, a digital media suite, and a cinema.

Across our varied creative spaces we bring 300 shows, events and films to our audiences each year, alongside a busy programme of over 250 courses and workshops. To improve access and representation of young people within the arts, South Hill Park also supports a group of young producers, aged between 14 and 25 years, who plan and devise arts activities and provision for other young people in the local area.

South Hill Park collaborates with theatre makers and companies in a variety of ways. The artistic vision of the centre includes the support and development of, and collaboration with many of its associate companies including its resident company Blackeyed Theatre Company. Many of these touring productions begin their artistic inception and development at South Hill Park. South Hill Park also works closely with its other associate companies including Chrysalis, Hit the Mark, Luke Brown, Peer Productions, Single Shoe Productions and Theatre Re. Partnerships are vital in the arts, and South Hill Park is fortunate to have Blackeyed Theatre as a partner.

To find out more sign up to our newsletter:
www.southhillpark.org.uk

South Hill Park Trust Limited
Registered Charity No: 265656

South Hill Park Arts Centre
Ringmead
Berkshire, RG12 7PA

Programme notes

I don't think I know anyone over the age of, say, ten, who doesn't know at least the name Sherlock Holmes. Conan Doyle's creation is part of the literary fabric of the country; his many cases and singular style – not to mention his relationship with Dr. Watson – a blueprint for countless novels, films, TV shows and theatre. That was one of the challenges that drew me to this adaptation; how might I interpret that relationship? What do we keep; what do we change? As it turned out, very little – when it comes to Holmes and Watson you don't mess with a winning formula!

Another thing that fascinated me, being a huge fan of crime fiction, was how to put a novel like this on stage without it becoming slow and unwieldy. Our intention from the beginning was to keep the action live; keep it flowing – have the audience see the case unfold and figure it out at almost the same time Holmes himself does. I think the way we've approached the story will appeal to fans of the novel and those who simply enjoy a rattling good crime story.

Collaboration has always been part of my process as a director - it's great to work with a bunch of people willing to throw in ideas, whether about staging, characterisation or the addition of musical underscore. This cast are no exception - they've really risen to the challenge and have probably come up with all your favourite bits!

On music (and with regard to collaboration), I'm delighted to be working with Tristan Parkes again. We've put countless shows together over the past twenty-five years - his process is similar to my own; his music very responsive. In a production such as this, that kind of thing is vital.

We're really proud of the piece, and we hope Sir Arthur would approve... more than that though, we hope you have a cracking time. The game is afoot!

Nick Lane | Writer & Director

Dramatis Personae

ACTOR ONE
Playing   Mr. Sherlock Holmes, *a consulting detective*

ACTOR TWO
Playing   Dr. John Watson, *a companion*
Also playing: HOLLIS (a courier)

ACTOR THREE
Playing   Miss Mary Morstan, *a governess*
Also playing: MRS. HUDSON (a housekeeper), MRS. SMITH (a boat merchant's wife)

ACTOR FOUR
Playing   Mr. Thaddeus Sholto, *a benefactor*
Also playing: WILLIAMS (a coach driver), SHOLTO (a Major), SHERMAN (a dog-handler), THOMAS (a Corporal)

ACTOR FIVE
Playing   Mr. Dost Akbar, *one of the four*
Also playing: SOLDIER (a soldier), ADNAN (a servant), CHOWDAR (a servant), ATHELNEY-JONES (an Inspector), KHAN (one of the four)

ACTOR SIX
Playing   Mr. Jonathan Small, *one of the four*
Also playing: MORSTAN (a Captain), MCMURDO (a prize-fighter), MATTHEWS (a Constable)

This adaptation was commissioned by Blackeyed Theatre Company to be performed internationally throughout 2018 and 2019. The production was directed by Nick Lane. All original music was written by Tristan Parkes in London, England.

Act One. *The stage is an abstract, modular space – representative of multi-locations, both interior and exterior. Four chairs sit behind a series of structures that make up the back section of the set – skeletal and blackened; a mixture of what looks like smashed and exposed beams and ornate Indian screens. Three open doorways sit within the back wall. On stage are four octagonal tables, rather Indian in their style; two smaller and taller, two wide and flat. There are four chairs and three movable columns that reflect the style of the rear section. At the top of the show one of the smaller tables is set downstage right with a chair next to it. On the table is a little case, not dissimilar in size to a glasses case Music plays as the audience enter; something with an Eastern influence; a touch mysterious and hypnotic. At FOH clearance the music changes. One by one the actors – all but HOLMES and WATSON – enter, finding positions within the space and playing the overture. Over this we hear recorded snippets of dialogue; parts of SMALL's story, some laughter... a dog barking, police whistles – possibly a gunshot. At a change in the music, HOLMES enters. He wears neither shoes nor socks, and though he has trousers on his top half is covered by a silken robe. He looks exhausted. He picks up the case, opens it and removes a syringe. Another change in the music. WATSON enters. He looks at HOLMES, watching him lift a sleeve of his robe, prepare his arm and push the needle into it. As he depresses the plunger the music calms. Over this, WATSON says:*

WATSON   *(To audience)* The Sign of Four. A Sherlock Holmes mystery by Dr. John Watson.

Lights gradually change – the suggestion being that it is no longer late at night; it is mid-morning. The music ceases and the other actors retreat to the seats behind the set. We hear the sounds of a

Victorian street. HOLMES' pained expression is replaced by one of serene contentment.

One week earlier...

WATSON looks at HOLMES, shakes his head and moves to hook his walking stick to a part of the set. Without opening his eyes, HOLMES says:

HOLMES   You don't need to say it.

WATSON   I wasn't going to say anything.

HOLMES   There's a glottal noise that you make when you are displeased.

WATSON   Is there?

HOLMES   Imperceptible to most, I'd imagine. Loud as a Gatling gun to me.

A beat.

Out with it.

WATSON   It's nothing, I...

A beat. WATSON moves a chair to join HOLMES, saying as he does so:

Which is it today? Morphine or cocaine?

HOLMES opens his eyes and looks languidly at his companion.

HOLMES   Cocaine. A seven percent solution. Would you care to try it?

HOLMES sees in WATSON's face that he would not.

19

As you wish.

WATSON opens his mouth to speak.

I'm aware of its secondary action. I simply find it so transcendentally stimulating. Besides... I'm bored.

He leans back into his armchair. WATSON addresses the audience.

WATSON   *(To audience)* It had long been the fashion of Sherlock Holmes to reach for the needle on occasions when there was nothing to otherwise occupy his mind.

HOLMES   I abhor the dull routine of existence.

WATSON   *(To audience)* He would say.

HOLMES   I crave mental exaltation.

WATSON   And you get that from, from... *(the needle)*

HOLMES   Partly. My unique profession provides the bulk of it.

WATSON   I'm not sure you can claim to be the only detective in the world.

HOLMES   The only unofficial *consulting* detective. When Gregson or Lestrade or that buffoon Athelney-Jones are out of their depths – which, by the way, is their usual state – the matter is laid before me.

WATSON   *(Amused)* And you solve it for them?

HOLMES looks at WATSON. He should know this.

HOLMES   How many games have we played out together?

WATSON   More than I can remember.

HOLMES   And how often have I been outwitted?

A beat.

So. There it is. They ask for my help, I pronounce a specialist's opinion which invariably brings the matter to an end.

WATSON   With the Inspectors' own deductive reasoning not figuring at all?

HOLMES   Rarely.

WATSON barks out a laugh.

This isn't ego, Watson. The work itself is my highest reward. My name figures in no newspapers. I claim no credit.

HOLMES picks up a series of papers (a tiny booklet), on the front of which is written "A Study in Scarlet." WATSON turns to the audience.

WATSON   *(To audience)* This was true to an extent, though he rather disliked the brochures I had had published describing his endeavours. Not, however, because he preferred his name to remain out of the limelight...

HOLMES   I glanced over this, by the way.

WATSON   Oh?

HOLMES   I can't congratulate you upon it.

WATSON looks knowingly at the audience as HOLMES elaborates.

Detection is, or ought to be, an exact science. It should be treated in the same manner. Your romantic embellishments are entirely unnecessary.

WATSON   In other words, every one of my pamphlets should be devoted solely to your own special doings.

HOLMES   Yes.

WATSON   And that isn't ego?

HOLMES   No. Facts are facts. Anything else is irrelevant.

WATSON   The readers would disagree.

HOLMES   The readers are wrong.

WATSON   As would I.

HOLMES   Then you're wrong too.

WATSON   I see.

HOLMES   I'm not sure you do. Here, in this section, you appear to suggest that observation and deduction are the same thing.

WATSON   No; merely that the one implies the other.

22

HOLMES   Not in the slightest.

He reaches for his pipe.

If you'd like I shall prove it.

WATSON   What I'd like is for you to put some shoes and socks on – it's eleven-thirty in the morning for heaven's sake. We're gentlemen of London, not savages.

HOLMES   *(Ignoring WATSON's plea) Observation* shows me that you have been to the Wigmore Street Post Office this morning. *Deduction* lets me know that while there you despatched a telegram.

WATSON   Right on both counts, but…

HOLMES   You have a little reddish mould adhering to your instep. Opposite the Wigmore Street Office they have taken up the pavement and thrown up some earth of a peculiar tint found nowhere else in the neighbourhood. If one is intending to use the Post Office it is nigh on impossible to avoid. So much is observation. The rest… is *deduction.*

WATSON   Go on.

HOLMES   I knew you hadn't written a letter since I sat opposite you all morning. I see also in your open desk there that you have a sheet of stamps and a thick bundle of postcards. So what else could you go into the post office for, if not to send a wire? Eliminate all other factors and the one which remains...

WATSON ...must be the truth.

HOLMES There. See? Done.

A beat.

Bored again.

HOLMES begins to prepare another syringe as WATSON turns to the audience.

WATSON *(To audience)* As fine a friend as Holmes could be, his dogmatic tone did rather grate on occasion, and so, to his lessons on deduction and observation, I intended to add one of my own – in humility. I wonder, I said, if I might put your theories to a more severe test.

WATSON produces a watch. HOLMES puts down the syringe.

HOLMES By all means.

WATSON *(To audience)* Holmes replied.

HOLMES It will prevent me from taking a second dose.

WATSON You say it's difficult to have any object in daily use without leaving your individuality upon it.

HOLMES I did.

WATSON   Well, I have here a watch which has recently come into my possession.

HOLMES   And you wish for me to tell you about the late owner.

WATSON   If you can.

There's a knock at the door. HUDSON enters.

HOLMES   Ah, Mrs. Hudson! Just in time to see me confound our dear doctor!

HUDSON   I can do that, sir. Takes no doing.

WATSON   What?

HUDSON   The spotted dog incident...?

WATSON   Ah. That... that was an honest mistake...

HOLMES   What's this?

HUDSON   My lips are sealed, sir.

HOLMES   Watson...?

WATSON   No... I shan't. No.

HOLMES   I'll have it out of you eventually.

HUDSON   Not now though, Mr. Holmes, sir. I have a lady downstairs asking for you.

HUDSON hands a card to HOLMES.

HOLMES   *(Reading)* "Miss Mary Morstan." Hmmm... not a name I'm familiar with.

HUDSON	Shall I send her up, sir?
HOLMES	Hold her for a moment, would you? I have confounding to do.
HUDSON	For the knock, sir?
HOLMES	For the knock.
HUDSON	Very good.

She exits, looking knowingly at WATSON.

WATSON	*(Calling after HUDSON)* And bring him some footwear!

A beat.

	(To HOLMES) Honestly, she's making it up.
HOLMES	Your crimson cheeks tell a different tale.
WATSON	Never mind that. The watch.

HOLMES turns the watch over in his hands.

HOLMES	There are hardly any data. The watch has been recently cleaned.
WATSON	That's right. Before it was sent to me.
HOLMES	It robs me of my most suggestive facts... but I'll make you a deal. If I illustrate my findings for you, will you reveal the truth behind the spotted dog?
WATSON	Never.
HOLMES	Well then...

He hands the watch back to WATSON and sits back in his chair. A beat.

WATSON   Confound you, Holmes. All right. You first.

HOLMES stands, a slight smile on his face. He retrieves the watch and looks at it.

HOLMES   To begin with I'd say the watch belonged to your eldest brother, who inherited it from your father.

WATSON   From the monogram on the back.

HOLMES   Partly. The watch is nearly fifty years old, and the initials are as old as the watch so it was made for the last generation. Jewellery usually descends to the eldest son, and he is most likely to have the same name as your father. But... what of him?

HOLMES turns the watch over in his hands.

He was a careless man; left with good prospects but threw them away. He lived for some time in poverty with occasional short intervals of prosperity before finally taking to drink and dying.

He hands the watch back to WATSON.

That's all I can gather.

WATSON   *(Upset)* How *could* you?

HOLMES   You just saw how I could, and I did. It's all there.

WATSON   No! You did not get all that from a watch. Somehow you've, you've found out about my brother. Stored the facts in that head of yours.

HOLMES   To what end?

WATSON   To, to, to... I don't know, but it's bad form, Holmes. It's charlatanism.

HOLMES   Not in the slightest. I swear I didn't know you had a brother until mere moments ago. Still, I viewed it as an abstract problem, quite forgetting how personal and painful it all might be. My apologies.

WATSON   Yes... well... it. Er; it, it... how could you have been so accurate?

HOLMES   Look at the watch and you'll see.

WATSON turns it over in his hands.

I stated your brother was careless. Now look at the lower part of the watch-case; dinted in two places and cut and marked all over from the habit of keeping coins or keys in the same pocket. Anyone who treats a fifty-guinea watch in such a way must be a careless man.

WATSON   I see.

HOLMES   Pawnbrokers in England, when they take a watch, they scratch the number of the ticket with a pin upon the inside of the case. I see four such numbers on the inside of this case.

28

This tells us, one, that your brother was often at low water and two, that he had occasional bursts of prosperity.

WATSON   When he bought the watch back. Of course.

HOLMES   Finally, look at the key-hole. See the thousands of scratches all around the hole? You'll never see a drunkard's watch without them.

WATSON puts the watch back in his pocket.

WATSON   I should have had more faith, Holmes. You were correct in every aspect.

HOLMES   Ah! Well, that was good luck. I could only say what was the balance of probability.

WATSON   None of it guesswork?

HOLMES   No, no; I never guess. Shocking habit – destructive to the logical faculty. Would you do the honours?

WATSON   I'm sorry?

HOLMES   Miss Morstan. The knock.

WATSON   Oh; of course.

WATSON bangs on the floor with his walking stick, then moves his chair to a position more able to accommodate guests. HOLMES takes the needle case from the table and, reaching through a gap in the back wall, puts it on a shelf behind the set. As they do this:

Do you imagine this to be a professional enquiry?

HOLMES One can but hope. My cache of narcotics has been severely depleted of late. I cannot live without brain work.

WATSON You can live without shoes though, apparently.

HOLMES What is the use of having powers without a field upon which to exercise them? What else is there to live for?

WATSON Love?

HOLMES At best, fleeting. At worst, dangerous. Fortunately we are safely removed from such untidiness here.

WATSON Yes, I rather fear we...

MARY enters, carrying a case of letters and a small cardboard box.

...are.

A beat. WATSON and MARY are staring at one another.

MARY *(To WATSON)* Mr... Holmes?

WATSON Sorry?

MARY Are... are you...?

WATSON I... er... no; I...

HOLMES I am he.

MARY   Apologies.

HOLMES   Not at all. Please, sit.

MARY sits. As she does so:

WATSON   *(To audience)* I had never in my life looked upon a face so delightful. Her expression was sweet and amiable and her large eyes singularly spiritual and sympathetic.

WATSON has moved to stand behind HOLMES' chair.

                  Once settled, she began…

MARY   You once helped my employer with a domestic complication, and she recommended you as a man of kindness and skill.

HOLMES   Ah… that would be Mrs. Cecil Forrester. And you are her governess.

MARY   That's… correct. How did…?

HOLMES   I believe I was of some slight service to Mrs. Forrester, though it was a very simple case as I recall.

MARY   She didn't think so. And you certainly can't say the same of my situation.

HOLMES visibly perks up upon hearing this.

HOLMES   Oh…?

MARY   I can hardly imagine anything more strange.

HOLMES, with a glance at WATSON, sits forward.

HOLMES   State your case.

WATSON   You will excuse me.

WATSON makes to leave.

MARY   *(To HOLMES)* I wonder if your friend would
be good enough to stop.

*HOLMES and WATSON look at one another, then WATSON
returns. HOLMES encourages MARY to begin. Music.
MORSTAN, MARY's father, enters in military uniform. He
stands on one of the lower tables and is very much part of MARY's
story as opposed to being with her physically. He holds a baby in
his arms, looking at her tenderly.*

I was born in India. My father was an Officer
there; he fought during the rebellion of '57.
My mother died when I was in my infancy,
and though I am told he doted upon me, the
volatility of the region forced him to make
what I can only imagine was a hard choice.

*Another man enters; an Indian SOLDIER in the service of the
British. As MARY's story continues, MORSTAN kisses the
child then carefully hands her over to the SOLDIER, who nods and
exits.*

He sent me back to London, in the care of
family friends, and when I was old enough –
having no relatives in this part of the world –
I was dispatched to a boarding school in the
North of England. There I remained until I
was seventeen, at which time I began a

32

correspondence with a father I barely remembered.

MORSTAN removes a letter from his tunic, opens it and reads, smiling to himself as he does so.

Over time the tone of these letters changed from formal and indifferent to kind and loving. Then, almost ten years ago my father, by now the Senior Captain of his regiment, telegraphed me that he had been granted twelve months' leave, and, more than that, he had arrived in London. He directed me to come down at once, giving the Langham Hotel as his address.

MORSTAN   There is much to discuss – I have a childhood to make up for and a lifetime to do it in. I return to you with a heart full of hope, to find peace, and comfort, and you. Please hurry. With love. Father.

MORSTAN exits. Lights.

MARY   On reaching the Langham I was informed that he had gone out the night before but had not returned. I waited all day without news. On the advice of the hotel manager I communicated with the police and the next morning we advertised in all the newspapers. From that day to this, no word has ever been heard of... of my unfortunate... father...

33

She fights back tears. WATSON offers a handkerchief but she has her own. HOLMES, on the other hand, removes a notebook.

HOLMES   The date?

MARY   Of the disappearance? The third of December, 1878.

HOLMES   Luggage?

MARY   Nothing of note; clothes, books and a number of curiosities from the Andaman Islands. He'd been one of the officers in charge of the convict-guard there.

HOLMES   Had he friends in town?

MARY   Only one that we know of – Major Sholto, from the same regiment, though he'd retired some time before and lived in Upper Norwood.

HOLMES   You contacted him, of course?

MARY   *(Nods)* He wasn't aware his brother officer was even in England.

A beat. HOLMES completes his notes.

HOLMES   A singular case.

MARY   That isn't the peculiar part.

She removes a newspaper clipping from the case and passes it to HOLMES.

On the 4th May 1882 an advertisement appeared in the Times asking for my address, stating it would be to my advantage to come forward. By my employers' advice I published my address... and that same day there arrived through the post a small cardboard box containing a very large and lustrous pearl. See for yourself.

She hands the box over to HOLMES. WATSON looks as HOLMES removes one of the pearls contained within.

HOLMES   A fine quality to be sure.

WATSON   There are half a dozen here.

MARY   Every year on the same day another pearl arrives, with no clue as to the sender.

HOLMES   No note?

MARY shakes her head. HOLMES passes back the box.

Most interesting.

WATSON   But...

A beat. HOLMES and MARY look at WATSON.

If I might ask... what drew you here today? We are some way past May.

MARY   This morning I received a letter. Here.

She takes a letter from the case and hands it to HOLMES.

HOLMES   Hmmm... postmark London SW. Date, September 7th. Man's thumb-mark on corner... probably postman.

He removes the letter. Lights up on a panel in the back wall of the set – a section of Indian screen, through which can be seen a face – that of THADDEUS. He speaks as the others look at the letter.

THADDEUS   Be at the third pillar from the left outside the Lyceum Theatre tonight at seven o'clock. If you are distrustful, bring two friends. You are a wronged woman and shall have justice. Do not bring police. Your unknown friend.

Lights down on the panel. THADDEUS moves back to his seat behind the set. HOLMES hands the letter back to MARY.

HOLMES   A very pretty little mystery. What do you intend to do, Miss Morstan?

MARY   That's what I wanted to ask you.

HOLMES   Then we'll most certainly go. You have no exception to Dr. Watson accompanying us? He's worked with me before.

MARY   *(With a look at WATSON)* None at all; if you are willing.

HOLMES   It's settled then. We'll take a cab to the Lyceum and meet you by the column in question. Ten minutes to seven; no later.

MARY   You're both very kind.

HOLMES   One last thing, Miss Morstan. Is there any resemblance between the hand in the letter and that of your father?

MARY   None at all.

HOLMES   I expected as much. Until later.

MARY   Mr. Holmes. Dr. Watson.

She stands, smiles at both of them and exits. A beat.

WATSON   What a thoroughly attractive woman.

HOLMES   I did not observe.

WATSON   I swear there is something positively inhuman in you at times.

HOLMES   Never allow your judgment to be biased by personal qualities. A client is a factor in a problem; nothing more.

WATSON   I'd say you were pulling my leg but I know you're not.

HOLMES   Not at all. Look at you.

WATSON   What about me?

HOLMES   Everything is unfocused. Emotional qualities are more antagonistic to clear reasoning than any other obstacle.

WATSON   In this case, however –

HOLMES   I never make exceptions. An exception disproves the rule. I'm going out. I have references to make.

WATSON   What shall I do?

HOLMES   Prepare for tonight. I shall be back in an hour.

He moves to the exit, then turns, smiling.

At which time I expect to be told the full tale of the spotted dog...

He exits. Music. WATSON turns to the audience.

WATSON   *(To audience)* As if a terrible malady had been lifted, Holmes was at once his best and sharpest self. Within moments he was fully dressed and out of the door at 221B Baker Street, heading for God knows where... while I, as ever when accompanying my friend, prepared myself for God knows what...

Music. The stage is reconfigured; three of the tables stacked centrally to form a column. HOLMES and WATSON stand by it. WATSON looks at his watch. Lights.

Is she late?

HOLMES   No; we're before our time.

WATSON   Damn watch...

HOLMES   Although I fear it may have been a wasted journey for all of us.

WATSON	You've solved it already?
HOLMES	Well... I've discovered a very suggestive fact.
WATSON	Why didn't you tell me before we left Baker Street?
HOLMES	How could I? I barely saw you – the unnecessary shaving, the careful choosing of clothes, of cologne...
WATSON	You told me to prepare for tonight.
HOLMES	I meant bring your revolver.
WATSON	Did you?
HOLMES	Yes!
WATSON	Oh.

A beat.

HOLMES	Besides, anything divulged there would only need repeating to Miss Morstan.
WATSON	Of course; I simply... thought...
HOLMES	Go on.
WATSON	Oh, it doesn't matter. You're right; she's a unit. A factor. In any event, what would she see in an ex-army surgeon with a weak leg and an even weaker bank account?
HOLMES	What indeed?

A beat.

WATSON   You really are no comfort at all, do you know that?

HOLMES spots MARY approaching.

HOLMES   Ah! Here she is now.

MARY enters. WATSON straightens up as best he can.

MARY   Gentlemen.

WATSON   Miss Morstan.

MARY   Again, I really can't thank you enough.

HOLMES   The Doctor and I were just discussing your case.

WATSON   *(Surprised)* We were?

HOLMES looks at WATSON, who alters the stress of his previous statement and says:

          (To MARY) We were.

HOLMES   It would seem that your Major Sholto, late of the 34th Bombay infantry, died at his home in Upper Norwood on the 28th of April, 1882.

MARY   Oh?

HOLMES   You said Major Sholto is the only person in London with whom your father could have visited, yet he denied having heard of your father's return. Then, *within a week of his death,* you receive a valuable present, repeated year after year and finally culminating in this letter describing you as a wronged woman. What wrong can it refer to except the deprivation of your father?

MARY   I'm sorry; I don't follow.

HOLMES   Who else but Sholto's heir would know anything about this mystery? Or wish to make compensation?

MARY   I hadn't considered that. I know that the Major and papa were friends. He was mentioned in a number of his letters. They were in command of the troops at the Andaman Islands, you see. Oh; which reminds me... I meant to bring this with me earlier, but...

She hands WATSON a piece of paper. In the distance a clock chimes the hour of seven.

HOLMES   What is it?

WATSON   A map of some kind, by the looks.

At this, WILLIAMS, a coach driver, enters. HOLMES draws but conceals a revolver.

HOLMES   Look sharp, doctor – this is our man.

WATSON conceals the piece of paper as WILLIAMS makes his approach.

WILLIAMS   Are you the parties that come with Miss Morstan?

MARY   I am Miss Morstan; these two gentlemen are
                  my friends.

WILLIAMS briefly scrutinises both HOLMES and WATSON.

WILLIAMS   You must excuse me, miss, but I was to ask
                  you to give your word that neither of your
                  companions is a police officer.

MARY   You have it.

WILLIAMS   Very well, Miss.

*WILLIAMS puts his fingers to his lips and whistles. Music – the
stage is reconfigured slightly; all four tables now combined to form
a carriage onto which HOLMES, WATSON and MARY all sit.
Lights close in on the three of them as the remaining actors play
music that creates atmosphere and the idea of travel. WATSON
addresses the audience.*

WATSON   *(To audience)* We had hardly taken our
                  places before the driver whipped up his horse
                  and we plunged away at a furious pace...

*The recorded sound of horse hooves replaces the music and the
musicians move backwards, retreating to their seats at the rear of
the set.*

HOLMES   Now, let's look at that map, shall we?
                  Watson?

WATSON   Here.

*WATSON passes the map over. HOLMES puts on his double-
lens glasses. They all look.*

HOLMES   Hmmm... *(Reading)* "3.37 from left."

MARY	Co-ordinates, I would imagine.
WATSON	Yes, but to what?
HOLMES	*(To MARY)* Where did you find this?
MARY	Is it important?
HOLMES	It was to your father.
MARY	It was with the other items from the Andaman Islands.
HOLMES	Not always... it has been kept in a pocket-book for a long time. At some time it has been pinned to a board, too. And look here!
WATSON	Where?
HOLMES	Just below the plan of the building; there... in pencil. See?
MARY	It's very faint...
WATSON	Part of the map?
HOLMES	A pattern, more like. Four crosses with their arms touching. And writing. *(Reading)* "The Sign of Four – Jonathan Small, Mahomet Singh, Abdullah Khan, Dost Akbar."

He removes the double-lens glasses and hands the paper back to MARY.

Preserve this carefully, Miss Morstan. It could prove useful. There may be more to this matter than first supposed. I must reconsider my ideas...

The carriage lurches. WATSON addresses the audience.

WATSON   *(To audience)* From that point on, Miss Morstan and myself alone conversed. At first I had some idea as to the direction we were driving but soon lost my bearings. Holmes seemed clear on our destination of course, muttering street names as the cab rattled on...

HOLMES   *(Eyes closed)* Rochester Row... now Vincent Square. Now we come out onto the Vauxhall Bridge. We are making for the Surrey side, apparently. You should be able to see the river now.

MARY   How does he do that?

WATSON   *(To audience)* Our cab dashed on.

HOLMES   Wordsworth Road. Priory Road.

WATSON   *(To audience)* Taking us out of the fashionable districts...

HOLMES   Lark Hall Lane. Stockwell Place.

MARY   It's remarkable.

WATSON   *(To audience)* ...before settling in a questionable and forbidding neighbourhood.

HOLMES   Robert Street. Cold Harbour Lane.

WATSON   *(To audience)* At last the cab drew up at the third house in a new terrace; one part of the monster tentacles that London was throwing out into the country.

HOLMES, WATSON and MARY step away from the created coach. Music echoing the earlier theme is played. The actors onstage, joined by the actor playing ADNAN, change the shape onstage, creating what looks like a reception room. At the end of the reconfiguration ADNAN bows to the guests and says:

ADNAN   Might I take your outer wear?

HOLMES   I'm quite comfortable, thank you.

WATSON   As am I.

A voice from offstage calls out:

THADDEUS   *(Off)* Show her into me, khitmutgar. Show her straight into me.

ADNAN smiles politely at the guests.

MARY   *(To WATSON)* Is that his name? I didn't quite catch it.

WATSON   Khitmutgar? No; khitmutgar means servant.

ADNAN   You speak Hindi, sir?

WATSON   *(In Hindi)* A little. *(In English; for MARY's benefit)* A little. My Persian is better. Oh; er... *(in Persian)* My Persian is better.

ADNAN   Your Hindi is better than my Persian

WATSON	Your English is better than both. *(To MARY)* I served in India and Afghanistan.
MARY	How wonderful!
WATSON	I'm not sure how wonderful it was; I took a jezail bullet in the leg...
MARY	I meant your skill in languages.
WATSON	Oh. Yes. Of course.
HOLMES	*(To ADNAN)* Your name, sir?
ADNAN	Adnan.
HOLMES	Settler.
ADNAN	Sir?
HOLMES	Your name. It means "to stay; abide."

He moves closer to ADNAN.

	(Confidentially) If I were to abide here, I would make sure the "Sahib" knew at least enough manners to use my name.
ADNAN	Thank you, sir.
THADDEUS	*(Off)* Khitmutgar! What the blazes...?

THADDEUS enters and sees the gentlemen with MARY.

	Oh! I'm... oh! Your servant, Miss Morstan. *(To HOLMES)* Your servant, sir. *(To WATSON)* Your servant. *(To ADNAN)* Khitmutgar; please put on a pot of tea.

ADNAN   At once, Sahib.

Nodding to all guests, he exits quickly. THADDEUS turns back to the guests, though he addresses MARY predominantly.

THADDEUS   Your servant; your servant. Welcome to my sanctum. A small place, miss, but furnished to my liking. An oasis of art in the howling desert of South London. If you would like to accompany me…

MARY   Might I first be permitted to know your name?

THADDEUS   Oh! Yes; I… where are my… *(manners)*? Thaddeus. Mr. Thaddeus Sholto. That is my name. You are Miss Morstan, of course. And these gentlemen…?

MARY   This is Mr. Sherlock Holmes, and this is Dr. Watson.

THADDEUS   *(To WATSON)* Ah! A doctor! Your servant; your servant. Have you your stethoscope?

WATSON   Not with me, alas.

THADDEUS   Not to worry; I have two. I have grave doubts as to my mitral valve.

THADDEUS puts his hand in his pocket and produces a Pinard stethoscope which he hands to WATSON.

                 If you would be so good.

WATSON   Oh; er…

WATSON listens to THADDEUS' heart for a moment.

It appears to be normal.

THADDEUS   Really?

WATSON nods and hands the stethoscope back to THADDEUS.

Hmmm. I've long had suspicion about that valve.

WATSON   I swear you have no cause for uneasiness.

THADDEUS   There's always cause for uneasiness. Everyone knows that. Your father knew it better than most, Miss Morstan.

MARY   "Knew?"

THADDEUS   That's right; God rest him.

An awkward pause. WATSON looks to see if MARY is okay. She is clearly upset at both the news and the manner of its delivery.

Oh, Miss; my humblest, most sincere...

MARY   I knew in my heart he was dead.

She takes a moment to compose herself.

What do you know of... of my father's passing?

THADDEUS   Much. I'll give you every information. And what's more, I can do you justice. Whatever Brother Bartholomew might say.

WATSON   I'm sorry; who?

THADDEUS   He's my twin.

HOLMES   Identical; correct?

THADDEUS   Yes, though we're quite, quite different, so... and he hates publicity.

MARY   Publicity?

THADDEUS   Of any kind. That's why I wanted no police involvement.

MARY   I'm... I'm not quite sure I understand.

THADDEUS   You will. You all will, once I... and then we can show a bold front to Brother Bartholomew and... and, yes; justice will be yours. If you all can swear that – *(you will not disclose what you hear)*

HOLMES   Whatever you say will go no further.

WATSON nods in agreement.

THADDEUS   That is well; that is well! May I offer you a glass of wine; a... a Chianti, or... perhaps you'd like to take a moment to look at the paintings. As you see, I am partial to the modern French school. The house at Norwood is filled with Indian art; tapestries and so on, but I find them so dreary and – *(lacking in modern form)*

MARY   Mr. Sholto, I don't wish to appear rude...

THADDEUS   Never!

MARY   Only it's late, and since you brought me here to tell me something...

THADDEUS   Of course! And here I am, going on and on about silly things like wine and art. You will forgive me?

MARY nods.

                  I so rarely entertain, you see. My disposition, and... I'm doing it again, aren't I? Goodness knows this is going to take long enough.

HOLMES   How much longer?

THADDEUS   I couldn't say precisely. We shall certainly have to go to Norwood and see Brother Bartholomew. He's angry about my communication with you, Miss Morstan. I told him, I said, "It's the right thing to do, Barty," but he... when he's in a temper...

WATSON   Why the delay? Let's go at once; meet the fellow mob-handed.

THADDEUS   That would hardly do – I don't know what he'd say to that.

HOLMES   Lay the facts out, sir. We might discern what remains.

THADDEUS   Very well then... though I warn you – and you particularly, Miss Morstan – that this might not make for easy listening. Some sections may, may prove to be upsetting, and... I'll do my best to convey them...

A beat. Music.

As you have no doubt guessed, my father was Major John Sholto. He had prospered in India and, upon his retirement some eleven years ago, returned to England with a considerable sum of money, a large collection of valuable curiosities and a staff of native servants. With these advantages he built himself a house, Pondicherry Lodge in Upper Norwood, and lived in great luxury. Bartholomew and I were the only children.

MARY   Your mother?

THADDEUS   Died when Brother Bartholomew and I were very young.

MARY   I'm sorry to hear that.

THADDEUS   You're too kind. I... I remember reading about your father's disappearance. Barty and I often discussed the case with our father... never for a moment suspecting that he alone knew the truth. Though...

MARY   Go on.

THADDEUS   Perhaps we ought to have expected... there was something about father at that time. He was very fearful of going out alone, always employing two prize-fighters to act as porters at Pondicherry Lodge. Williams, who drove you tonight, was one of them.

MARY   What was he so afraid of?

THADDEUS   He never told, but he did have an aversion to men with wooden legs. On one occasion he actually fired his revolver at a wooden-legged man who proved to be a harmless tradesman.

HOLMES   Indeed?

THADDEUS   Yes... we had to pay a large sum just to hush the matter up.

A beat.

In early March of 1882, father received a letter from India. What was in it I could not tell you, but he nearly fainted upon reading it, and from that day he sickened to his death. In late April of that year we were informed by the family physician that he was beyond all hope and that he wished to make a final communication to us.

THADDEUS stands and moves to a seat in a different part of the space, though he does not immediately sit in it. It is almost now as if he is talking to himself as much as he is communicating with the group.

I remember... entering his room – I was in front of Barty... was I? Or was I... slightly behind him? Don't suppose that's important, but... yes, yes, there we were, and he was... he was sitting in this very chair, where it used to be, by the window in his study. He was breathing heavily. "Lock the door, boys," he said, "and come close to me." His voice had grown thin and there was an odour... if odours can be described as ... as sad, then this one... it was the smell of death, I suppose. He bade us sit, and... and he grasped our hands...

Lights flicker. Thunder rumbles. THADDEUS sits.

"I have only one thing which lies heavy on my mind," he said. "My treatment of poor Morstan's orphan."

WATSON   My God.

THADDEUS   "My greed; my blind, foolish avarice has withheld from her the treasure, at least half of which should have been hers."

MARY   Treasure?

THADDEUS   "Worse still, I have robbed her of peace concerning her father..."

There is the sound of knocking, as if at a door. Thunder again. Lights flicker once more. MARY stands. WATSON stands with her.

MARY   Oh, please tell me.

THADDEUS   We were suddenly children again, Barty and I. "Many nights I have listened to you speculate as to the whereabouts of my old friend Captain Morstan, when I alone could have told you everything."

MARY   What did he say?

WATSON   Enough theatrics. Tell her, man!

THADDEUS   "Listen now boys, for I am about to reveal
                  that which has laid my soul heavy these past
                  four years."

More thunder. Another light flicker.

                  "While in India, through circumstances too
                  complicated to go into, Captain Morstan and
                  I came into possession of a large treasure."

WATSON   Holmes?

HOLMES   Let him continue. Listen.

THADDEUS   "On the night he died, the Captain called
                  upon me to discuss it. It was a conversation I
                  was not looking forward to."

HOLMES   We are getting to it…

WATSON   How much more does Miss Morstan have to
                  hear…?

THADDEUS   "There was a storm in the air when Arthur
                  Morstan met his end. Howling wind, rain and
                  the ominous approach… of thunder."

*A huge roll of thunder. Lights flicker and snap to black. MARY
screams. Immediately HOLMES, WATSON and MARY exit
and Lal CHOWDAR, SHOLTO's manservant, enters. SHOLTO
is now played fully by THADDEUS. We hear a voice from
offstage.*

MORSTAN   *(Off)* John? John! I will not be kept out much longer!

Lights up.

CHOWDAR   Sahib?

SHOLTO   Let him in.

CHOWDAR nods and exits. SHOLTO removes from a drawer a revolver. He moves to a shelf, opens a box and takes from it a revolver. He checks it is loaded, sets it next to him and sits again. A moment later, MORSTAN enters, looking decidedly put out.

MORSTAN   Was that your idea of a joke? Leaving me out on a hellish...

The sentence trails as he sees the revolver.

SHOLTO   I know why you're here, Arthur.

MORSTAN   Evidently.

A beat. SHOLTO smiles.

SHOLTO   It's good to see you.

MORSTAN does not reply.

How's your heart?

MORSTAN   *(Ignoring the question)* What you did was not part of the arrangement.

SHOLTO snorts.

Call me old-fashioned, Major, but when one gives one's word...

SHOLTO   To a man like that?

MORSTAN   To any man!

A beat.

                   Where is it?

SHOLTO   Close by.

MORSTAN   And tell me; was I part of your plan, or were you set against me too?

SHOLTO   Never against you, Captain.

MORSTAN takes a step towards his old companion.

MORSTAN   Never…?

SHOLTO's hand rests lightly on the revolver.

SHOLTO   Not unless you force me to it.

A beat.

MORSTAN   It's like that, is it?

SHOLTO   It needn't be.

MORSTAN   Had we not been given that information – *(you would never have seen that treasure)*

SHOLTO   But we were.

MORSTAN   They shared with us – *(a great secret)*

SHOLTO   It wasn't theirs to share!

MORSTAN   Listen to me; I have travelled halfway around the world to try and talk some sense into you. Let us take what we agreed upon and no more. We can live well enough, and not spend the rest of our days constantly glancing over our shoulders.

SHOLTO   Look at this place. I've spent my share already.

MORSTAN   Then take it from mine!

SHOLTO   I won't steal from you.

MORSTAN   Yet you will from…

SHOLTO   Criminals? Yes.

MORSTAN   And that makes you *what*, exactly?

A beat. Thunder rumbles outside.

SHOLTO   You're shaking.

MORSTAN   I'm fine.

SHOLTO   Won't you sit?

MORSTAN   Is that an order?

SHOLTO   Oh, come on Arthur!

MORSTAN   Do what's right. I implore you.

SHOLTO   And break a quartet of men out of prison?

MORSTAN	Considering the fortune that put them there has paid for this house and more besides... yes.

A beat.

	They... they trusted us. They...
SHOLTO	My God, man; you look dreadful. Won't you stay the night? We can talk further in the morning.
MORSTAN	I can't. Mary is travelling down to see me. I have a room at the Langham.
SHOLTO	How many years has it been?
MORSTAN	All her life, practically. Tomorrow was to be the start of a new chapter. For both of us.
SHOLTO	It still can be.
MORSTAN	Not until you tell me you will honour the agreement made with the four.

A beat.

SHOLTO	Would you have me lie to you too?
MORSTAN	*(Bellowing)* No, I would have you behave like a gentleman!

Thunder rumbles. MORSTAN is all at once unsteady on his feet. He clutches his arm, grunting with discomfort. SHOLTO hasn't noticed.

SHOLTO   They will get not a penny from me, and it ill-
behoves your position to fight their corner!
Let that be an end to it!

With a groan, MORSTAN pitches forward towards the table.
Mistakenly thinking he is going for the gun, SHOLTO snatches it
up and levels it at his old friend, in time to see him crash to the
ground. Silence.

Arthur?

CHOWDAR enters.

CHOWDAR   Sahib! Are you… hurt…?

He quickly surveys the scene. Looks back at SHOLTO.

SHOLTO   It's… it's not…

CHOWDAR heads back to the exit.

Where are you going?

Nothing. SHOLTO drops the revolver on the table.

Chowdar! Chowdar!

CHOWDAR returns. He looks calmer.

CHOWDAR   The door is locked, Sahib. No-one need know
you have killed him.

SHOLTO   I didn't!

CHOWDAR   I heard it all, Sahib. I heard you quarrel, and
I heard the blow.

SHOLTO   No!

CHOWDAR   Do not fear. My lips are sealed.

SHOLTO   But I'm innocent; I swear it!

CHOWDAR   Sahib, if what I saw gave me reason to doubt it, why take your chances with a jury?

A beat. SHOLTO is considering this.

      All are asleep in the house. Let's hide him together and who is the wiser?

Silently SHOLTO nods his consent – he offers the revolver to CHOWDAR who takes it, nods, and tucks it into his belt. Lights dim a little. MORSTAN stands and exits, followed by CHOWDAR. At the same time, HOLMES, WATSON and MARY return and take their positions on the stage, listening to the end of THADDEUS' story. Another thunderclap, the lights flicker and SHOLTO's position in the chair becomes less physically strong, more slouched. Lights return to their previous state. SHOLTO is now talking to his two sons and on the verge of death.

SHOLTO   Thus persuaded, Lal Chowdar and I found a place to conceal the body. Where I shall not tell you, for I will not have my friend's eternal rest disturbed. Lal Chowdar died some years later, taking his secret with him to the grave. I swear I am blameless in Arthur's death. My fault lies in the fact we concealed not only the body, but also the treasure. I have clung onto all of it. Here; see...

He takes from the pocket of the robe a pearl chaplet complete with cross.

This – this chaplet. I took this from the box that very evening. Every night since I have asked myself why I would not simply surrender it to Arthur's daughter. I'm trusting you, my sons, to do what I could not. Give her a fair share of the Agra treasure once I am gone. Now... put your ears down to my mouth. The treasure is hidden in –

Sudden sting of music – a loud, dramatic stab. SHOLTO's mouth stands agape, jaw working soundlessly for a moment – he is clearly terrified. His eyes stare wildly, then he screams:

Keep him out! For Christ's sake, keep him out!

Music grows, then fades. SHOLTO becomes THADDEUS once more. He rejoins the guests.

(As THADDEUS) We searched the garden that night; the only sign of the intruder a single foot-mark in the flower bed under the window. The next morning, however... father's room had been ransacked. Nothing had been taken, but cupboards and boxes had been rifled, and upon his chest was fixed a torn piece of paper marked with the words 'The Sign of Four.'

MARY opens her mouth to speak; HOLMES holds up a hand to prevent it.

It took us years, and a lot of excited digging, to discover the treasure's location. And when we weren't digging we were arguing.

MARY Over what?

THADDEUS Over you, Miss Morstan. And the chaplet.

A beat.

To my mind we were your trustees, so finding your address and sending you a pearl at fixed intervals...

MARY It was kind of you.

THADDEUS I wouldn't see you destitute, Miss. Alas Brother Bartholomew didn't see it in that light, and in the end our differences became unbearable. I left Pondicherry Lodge, taking some odd items of furniture, the old khitmutgar and Williams with me and leaving him to find the treasure on his own.

HOLMES Adnan.

THADDEUS I'm sorry?

HOLMES His name is Adnan.

A beat.

THADDEUS A – Adnan; yes. Of course. I... Adnan and Williams came with me, and here we have stayed... then yesterday I learned that the treasure had been discovered. I instantly communicated with Miss Morstan, and now

62

all that remains is for us to drive out to Norwood and demand our share. I explained my views last night to Brother Bartholomew, so we shall be expected, if not welcome, visitors.

A beat.

HOLMES   You have behaved honourably, sir. In return, we should be able to shed some light on that which is still dark to you.

He stands.

Shall we?

THADDEUS   Indeed. *(Calling)* Khi – er; Adnan…? Prepare the carriage. *(To MARY)* We ride… to Pondicherry Lodge!

Music. WATSON addresses the audience as the stage is reconfigured.

WATSON   *(To audience)* The lateness of the hour and the grave circumstances of our journey played heavily on the minds of my companions, though I confess I was burdened with another trouble; one of the heart. En route to Upper Norwood Thaddeus had told us that the fortune awaiting Miss Morstan totalled a quarter of a million pounds. Overnight she would change from a needy governess to the richest heiress in England. And though it would ultimately take her away from me entirely – I became all the

63

more determined to help Miss Morstan—a feeling that grew as we arrived at Pondicherry Lodge...

The columns have been positioned to resemble gate posts, in front of which stands MCMURDO, a stern-faced man. WATSON, THADDEUS, HOLMES and MARY survey the scene from a distance, before:

MCMURDO Who's there?

THADDEUS No need to worry.

MCMURDO That you, Mr. Thaddeus?

THADDEUS It is.

MCMURDO Who are the others?

WATSON *(Quietly; to HOLMES)* I recognise that fellow.

THADDEUS Friends.

MCMURDO Mr. Bartholomew said nothing about no friends.

HOLMES *(Quietly; to WATSON)* So you should. He was middleweight Champion of England.

THADDEUS I told my brother to expect me.

MCMURDO I can't go against regulations, Sir. You know that.

THADDEUS Nonsense. Nonsense! Fetch my brother.

WATSON *(Quietly; to HOLMES)* Jack McMurdo?

HOLMES	*(Quietly; to WATSON)* The same.
MCMURDO	He'll only say what I said.
THADDEUS	Fetch him and find out.
MCMURDO	Sir, he ain't been out of his room all day and I won't disturb him.
MARY	*(Quietly)* Who is he?
WATSON	*(Quietly)* A prize-fighter.
MCMURDO	You can come in, but your friends will have to stay here.
THADDEUS	We have a young lady with us. She cannot be forced to stand on the public road at this hour.
WATSON	*(Quietly)* He was said to have the fiercest right hand in England.
MCMURDO	Your brother pays me well to do my duty, and my duty I'll do. I don't know none o' your friends, and I can't let in who I don't know.
HOLMES	But you do know me, McMurdo.

HOLMES steps out from behind THADDEUS.

WATSON	*(Whispering)* Holmes…!
MCMURDO	Stay back, sir…
HOLMES	You can't have forgotten me, surely.

MCMURDO   Stay back.

THADDEUS   There's no need for this…

MARY   What's happening?

HOLMES   I know you well enough.

MCMURDO   I'm warning you, sir.

THADDEUS   Stop!

HOLMES   You rarely plant your feet, and you swing wide; open yourself up on the left.

MCMURDO   What?

MARY   *(To WATSON)* What's he doing?

WATSON   I have no idea.

THADDEUS   Stop! *(Shouting)* Bartholomew!

HOLMES   It's why you couldn't beat Kilkeen back in '83…

MCMURDO   That's it!

MCMURDO takes a wide swing at HOLMES which he dodges with ease and turns on his heel, ready for the next swing. MCMURDO fires another shot; a straight left. HOLMES feints to the right and taps MCMURDO on the side below the ribs.

Don't insult me; fight!

MCMURDO takes two further swings which HOLMES avoids again, tapping MCMURDO on the side of the head after the second.

HOLMES   I already did. And on that occasion…

MCMURDO aims a body blow at HOLMES which connects. HOLMES collapses to his knees before saying:

I lasted the full three minutes…

MCMURDO stops. HOLMES looks up at him.

Alison's rooms. Your benefit, three years ago.

A beat.

MCMURDO   Not… not Mr. Sherlock Holmes?

HOLMES   What's left of him.

Laughing, MCMURDO offers a hand to help HOLMES to his feet.

MCMURDO   God's truth, how could I have mistook you? Why didn't you say something?

HOLMES   I did!

MCMURDO   My blood was up then, sir. I wasn't thinking. If you'd just stepped up and given me that cross-hit of yours under the jaw, I'd have known you without question.

HOLMES   Our friend won't keep us out in the cold now, I'm sure.

MCMURDO   In you come, sir. In you come.

MCMURDO steps to one side, ushering first HOLMES then MARY and THADDEUS through the gateposts. He returns to guard duty after this. WATSON watches them go, then turns to the audience.

WATSON   *(To audience)* Along with the life of the mind that Holmes lived as Consulting Detective were a number of more robust physical pursuits that, he would say, 'challenged his wider perceptions of excellence.' Pugilism was one of those. I advised him against it almost as often as I did the needle, but he was his own man, and –

Whatever WATSON was going to say is lost as a blood-curdling scream rips through the air. WATSON looks off; terrified.

          Good God!

Music ramps up. WATSON exits hurriedly. The stage is quickly reconfigured; WATSON and MCMURDO taking a gatepost each and moving them to the sides. THADDEUS enters and sits on a chair close to WATSON who, once he's positioned his column, turns and enters the scene with THADDEUS. MCMURDO exits.

          Who was that? I heard it from the street!

THADDEUS   The housekeeper, Mrs. Bernstone. Miss Morstan is sitting with her.

WATSON   What caused her to scream like that?

THADDEUS   I've no idea – my mitral valve...

WATSON   *(Sharply)* There's nothing wrong with –

A beat. He calms himself.

          Your mitral valve is fine.

THADDEUS   I do hope so.

WATSON   Where's Holmes?

THADDEUS	Upstairs. He asked me to stay down here and to wait for you.
WATSON	I see.
THADDEUS	I think he may be in with Brother Bartholomew, though I haven't heard any raised voices...

WATSON looks around him.

WATSON	What in heaven's name happened in here?
THADDEUS	The holes? That was us. Brother Bartholomew mostly. Awful, isn't it? Once we'd dug up the grounds we surmised that father must have walled up the treasure.
WATSON	And had he?
THADDEUS	In a manner of speaking. My brother discovered that the building was four feet higher than the interior would suggest. That was his breakthrough yesterday.
WATSON	The roof?
THADDEUS	Quite so.
WATSON	Perhaps Holmes is – *(talking it through with your brother)*

HOLMES enters.

HOLMES	Watson, I need you to come with me.
WATSON	What's going on? Is everything all right?
HOLMES	All will become clear.
WATSON	The scream?

HOLMES   That too. Come on.

THADDEUS   Mr. Holmes? Is it safe for me to...?

HOLMES   If I could beg your perseverance for just a few moments more.

THADDEUS   Your servant; your servant.

HOLMES   Thank you. *(To WATSON)* Watson; with me!

Lights. Music. THADDEUS stands – his expression changes; all nervousness gone – he is a neutral actor. HOLMES and WATSON stand behind him, and THADDEUS falls into their arms. They position him on the floor and WATSON chalks a line around him as HOLMES and the actor playing AKBAR reconfigure the space, creating what looks like a ransacked room – columns leaning against the back wall, upturned chairs and so on. HOLMES and WATSON then exit. The actor playing THADDEUS stands, places a small piece of paper near the hand and something where his ear might have been. He looks down at the outline and exits. The music steadies and we hear:

HOLMES   *(Off)* With me, Watson. After three. One... two... three!

The actors upstage create the sound of a door being smashed in, and HOLMES and WATSON spill out onto the stage, looking at the outline of the body. Music down to an ominous underscore.

WATSON   What is this place?

HOLMES   Bartholomew Sholto's private laboratory... and final resting place. It would seem that Mrs. Bernstone had been trying to rouse the master of the house all day. Moments before you arrived, she and I had managed to force the key out of the back of the door with a hairpin. The scream you heard was Mrs.

Bernstone seeing what you just have through
the keyhole.

WATSON   And Mary? Did she…?

HOLMES   No; she was spared. In truth Miss Morstan
has proved herself most useful. Without her
presence as a balm for the housekeeper, I fear
I would not have learned anything.

WATSON   What's that in his hand there?

*HOLMES leans forward and takes the note, handing it to
WATSON.*

              (Reading) "The Sign of Four." In God's
name, what does it all mean?

HOLMES   It means murder. *(Looking at the body)* Ah! I
expected it. Look, there – just above the ear.

WATSON looks.

WATSON   Looks like a thorn.

HOLMES   It is. Be careful when you remove it. It's
poisoned.

WATSON   Me? When *I* remove it?

*HOLMES looks at WATSON, who sighs and leans forward,
taking the thorn and holding it gingerly.*

              This is all growing darker instead of clearer.

HOLMES   On the contrary; it clears every instant. I only
require a few missing links to have an entirely
connected case.

WATSON   What now?

HOLMES   Now we need to inform…

At this point THADDEUS enters the room holding a lantern. He sees his brother.

THADDEUS   Barty! He...

HOLMES   Keep back, Mr. Sholto.

THADDEUS   But I... *(to WATSON)* is he...

WATSON nods. THADDEUS staggers backwards. He puts the lantern down.

No! No, he was strong! I'm the one with the weak mitral valve...

WATSON grits his teeth. HOLMES looks over at THADDEUS gravely.

HOLMES   It wasn't his heart, Mr. Sholto. I'm afraid your brother has been murdered.

THADDEUS   He...

A thought strikes him. He moves to a very specific place in the room, looks for something there, then turns; angry and upset in equal measure.

Oh, why did we ever look for that chest?

WATSON   The treasure?

THADDEUS   Gone! Stolen, no doubt. There in the ceiling is the hole through which we lowered it. I helped him to do it! I was the last person who saw him! I left him here last night, and I heard him lock himself in as I came downstairs.

HOLMES   What time was that?

THADDEUS   Ten o'clock. And now he's dead, and the police will be called in, and I'll be suspected of having had a hand in it. I will, won't I? I'm bound to be!

THADDEUS looks quickly from HOLMES to WATSON.

But... you don't think... surely you don't think I could have...? Is it likely I'd have brought you here if...?

HOLMES   Never fear, Mr. Sholto. Take my advice – go to the station and report this matter to the police. Offer to assist them in every way.

THADDEUS   To... assist...?

HOLMES   That's right. We shall wait here until your return.

THADDEUS   Assist. Very well. Thank you, gentlemen. Thank you so much!

THADDEUS exits. HOLMES turns to WATSON.

HOLMES   Now, we have some time to ourselves. Let's make good use of it. First things first; how did these folk come, and how did they go?

WATSON   Well... not through the door. It's not been opened since last night.

HOLMES   Window it is then.

HOLMES moves downstage and looks at the "window" – a section of the fourth wall..

(*Almost to himself*) Snibbed on the inside. Framework solid. No hinges at the side. Hmmm... no water-pipe near. Roof quite out

73

of reach, and yet... a man has been through this window.

WATSON   How can you tell that from here?

HOLMES   I *observed* the building's layout on my approach, and I *deduced* the rest from the print on the sill.

WATSON   All right; all right. I get it – the two are different.

HOLMES   And yet you're still to reveal the legend of the spotted dog.

WATSON   Surely this is not the time.

HOLMES   Indeed not. Come and look at this.

WATSON approaches.

There. A circular mark.

WATSON   What is that?

HOLMES   Can't you guess?

WATSON   Well... not a footmark...

HOLMES   Something far more valuable. *(Pointing) There* is the footmark... and *(pointing) there*, my dear Watson... is the impression of a wooden stump.

WATSON   My God... the wooden-legged man.

HOLMES   Quite so. And he had help.

WATSON   Did he?

HOLMES   Could you scale the outer wall here?

WATSON   Of course not. It's impossible.

HOLMES   And you have all limbs more or less intact. But suppose...

HOLMES moves to the rope.

          Just suppose you had a friend up here who lowered you a rope; hooking it to a beam. If you were an active man, you'd be straight up, wooden leg and all, and you'd depart in the same fashion.

WATSON   Ah, but then you'd leave the rope...

HOLMES   ...which your ally would draw up, untie, shut the window – snibbing it on the inside, naturally...

WATSON   Naturally...

HOLMES   ...before climbing down the way he originally came.

WATSON   That's all very well, but how did this ally get in?

HOLMES   Look around you.

WATSON   The door was locked, the window snibbed... the chimney?

HOLMES   The grate is too narrow.

WATSON   Then what...?

HOLMES   The clues are all there. Look at the body. The distortion of the face, the hardness of the muscles. What does that tell you?

WATSON	That a powerful vegetable alkaloid killed him. Strychnine, or something similar which would produce tetanus.
HOLMES	Holding him in position.
WATSON	That's right.
HOLMES	Next; the thorn. You still have it, yes?
WATSON	Oh, yes.
HOLMES	Describe it.
WATSON	Well... it's a black thorn; not English. It has a glazed look near the point.
HOLMES	Yes, yes; the strychnine. What else?
WATSON	The blunt end has been trimmed and rounded off with a knife.
HOLMES	Where did you take the thorn from?
WATSON	Behind the ear.
HOLMES	So... hit behind the ear... with a poison that paralyses before it kills...

A beat.

Come on; come on – when you have eliminated the impossible whatever remains, *however improbable*, must be the truth.

WATSON looks up.

WATSON	The hole in the ceiling...?
HOLMES	Excellent!

76

HOLMES climbs onto the tables which are positioned near the back wall.

> Hand me that lantern, would you?

WATSON   What are you doing?

HOLMES   Surveying the room in which the treasure was found...

Music. Raising the lantern, HOLMES peers through one of the gaps in the back wall created by the splintered wood.

WATSON   Anything?

HOLMES   A trapdoor which leads out onto the roof. That's where he gained entry. And a small footprint in the dust, the size of a child's.

WATSON   A child did it?

HOLMES   Unlikely.

HOLMES descends the makeshift ladders, places the lantern down and starts to move around the space..

> *(To himself)* Let's see now.

WATSON   *(To audience)* This was my old friend in his element. Back and forth he went, nose pressed close to the floor, drawing, sketching and muttering to himself. I confess that my mind wandered to the face of Miss Morstan more than once; her eyes, the kindness of her smile... her impending wealth and subsequent unavailability... damn you, John Watson; why do you think such things? Then –

HOLMES   A-ha!

WATSON   *(To audience)* Said Holmes with a start.

HOLMES   We're in luck. The accomplice has had the misfortune to tread in the creosote where the carboy has cracked. You can see the outline of the edge of his small foot here. Handkerchief, please.

WATSON   Oh; yes. Here.

HOLMES takes WATSON's handkerchief and smears it in the creosote before handing it back to WATSON.

HOLMES   *(To himself)* One for you, Toby.

WATSON   What? Who?

HOLMES   Never mind that now; I need you to –

There is a noise, as if from downstairs. HOLMES stops what he was saying abruptly.

              Hello! Sounds like we have company.

WATSON   Local Police?

HOLMES   Yes, and Athelney-Jones of the Yard.

WATSON   In Norwood? Don't be –

At this, ATHELNEY-JONES enters, followed closely by a nervous THADDEUS. He is slightly the worse for drink.

ATHELNEY-J.   Well well well. If it isn't the theorist!

HOLMES   Inspector.

ATHELNEY-J.   Haven't seen you since…

HOLMES   Bishopsgate.

ATHELNEY-J.   That's right.

HOLMES smiles.

	Put us on the right track there. Though… it was more luck than judgment.
HOLMES	Not at all. It was a piece of very simple reasoning.
ATHELNEY-J.	Never be ashamed to own up; that's what I say. *(To WATSON)* Evening, Wilson.
WATSON	Watson.
ATHELNEY-J.	That's it. So, what brings you here?
THADDEUS	Oh, they… were invited. By me.
HOLMES	We were accompanying Miss Morstan.
ATHELNEY-J.	Were you now? *Were* you now…?
WATSON	Just what are you suggesting?
ATHELNEY-J.	I'm not suggesting anything… yet. Anyway… bad business, this. Bad business. Door locked, man dead, half a million missing? Lucky I was out at Norwood on another case. *(Looking at the body)* Hello. He looks familiar. I've seen him somewhere before…
THADDEUS	He's my twin.
ATHELNEY-J.	That'll be it. *(To HOLMES)* What d'you think the man died of?
HOLMES	*(Dryly)* Oh, this is hardly a case for me to theorize over.
ATHELNEY-J.	Good.

MARY enters.

79

MARY Forgive me, Mr. Sholto…

THADDEUS Can I help?

ATHELNEY-J. Who's this now?

MARY The staff are terribly nervous. Mrs. Bernstone is beside herself.

ATHELNEY-J. What; is she a twin as well?

A beat.

Get it? Twin? Beside herself… never mind. Who are you, Miss?

WATSON This is Miss Mary Morstan.

ATHELNEY-J. I wasn't asking you, Wilson.

WATSON Watson!

ATHELNEY-J. Same. *(To MARY)* Now…

THADDEUS She's my guest. Like I said, the treasure is… well, it's… it's hers too.

ATHELNEY-J. Yes, yes. Good. Right. *(Calling off)* Constable! *(To HOLMES)* How was the window?

HOLMES Fastened; but there are steps on the sill.

ATHELNEY-J. Forget that then.

WATSON *(Shocked)* Forget the steps?

ATHELNEY-J. If the window was shut, yes.

WATSON Who was up there then?

ATHELNEY-J. Left by the window cleaner I expect.

WATSON   A window cleaner? With a wooden leg?

ATHELNEY-J. Calm down, Wilson.

WATSON   Watson!

ATHELNEY-J. *(To HOLMES)* You can tell who's the organ grinder.

A CONSTABLE enters.

          Here he is. What do they call you; Constable Slowcoach?

CONSTABLE   Matthews, sir.

ATHELNEY-J. Well, Constable "Matthews-sir," could you please make sure all the people in the house – servants and guests alike – are relaxed and comfortable.

CONSTABLE   Sir.

ATHELNEY-J. And do try to keep them in the same room.

CONSTABLE   Yes, sir.

CONSTABLE exits. ATHELNEY-JONES turns to THADDEUS.

ATHELNEY-J. Mr. Sholto, I wonder if you wouldn't mind returning downstairs for a spell? Go and calm down your staff.

THADDEUS   They were my brother's staff.

ATHELNEY-J. Will they know the difference?

WATSON   One of them's dead!

ATHELNEY-J. Keep your hair on, Wilson.

WATSON has to turn away to avoid shouting at ATHELNEY-JONES. MARY moves to WATSON and holds his hand.

> *(To THADDEUS)* If you wouldn't mind. Join the Constable. You too, Miss.

THADDEUS   Your servant; your servant.

THADDEUS exits. MARY squeezes WATSON's hand and follows. Once they are gone:

ATHELNEY-J.   I have a theory.

HOLMES   You do?

ATHELNEY-J.   See if you can get your famous brain round this – you too, Wilson.

WATSON   My name... is Watson.

ATHELNEY-J.   Hmm. *(To HOLMES)* Sholto was, on his own confession, with his brother last night. Correct?

HOLMES   As far as we know.

ATHELNEY-J.   There we are then. Brother dies in a fit, Sholto walks off with the treasure. How's that?

HOLMES   And of course upon his death Bartholomew gets up and locks the door on the inside...

ATHELNEY-J.   Yes!

ATHELNEY-JONES thinks about this for a moment.

> Ah. No. All right; let's go from the start. This Thaddeus Sholto *was* with his brother; there *was* a quarrel.

HOLMES   Correct.

ATHELNEY-J.   The brother is dead and the jewels are gone.

HOLMES   Yes.

ATHELNEY-J.   Now... no-one saw the brother from the time Thaddeus left him. His bed's not been slept in... and Thaddeus is evidently in a disturbed state of mind.

WATSON   He's a valetudinarian.

ATHELNEY-J.   I don't care what he eats. My net is closing in on him.

HOLMES   I'm afraid you're missing one or two rather pertinent facts, Inspector. Bartholomew Sholto was shot from above with a poison dart. Upon his body was left this card.

He shows the card to ATHELNEY-JONES.

How does that fit your theory?

ATHELNEY-J.   Perfectly! House is full of Indian curiosities. Thaddeus could have found a blow-pipe here.

HOLMES   He *could...*

ATHELNEY-J.   Could have fired it too. Brother's sitting down, he's behind him...

WATSON   What of the card then? "The Sign of Four." Hmm? What of that?

ATHELNEY-J.   Red herring. Intended to throw us off the scent. Well, it may have fooled you, Wilson, and the great Sherlock Holmes, but it'll take more than that to get past me. All I have to do now is work out how he escaped...

Eventually ATHELNEY-JONES looks up.

And there it is; the old 'hole in the ceiling' route. Let's have a look here...

ATHELNEY-JONES does the same as HOLMES did earlier, climbing up tables to peer into the loft space.

WATSON   Of all the detectives at Scotland Yard...

HOLMES   Fret not, Watson. *Il n'y a pas des sots si incommodes que ceux qui ont de l'esprit!*

ATHELNEY-JONES descends.

ATHELNEY-J.   You keep your theories, Mr. Holmes. I'll stick with what's in front of me... including the trap-door communicating with the roof. Spot that, did you?

HOLMES   Yes.

ATHELNEY-J.   Oh? Oh; you saw that? Yes; right – didn't have it down as the escape route though, did you?

HOLMES   *(Dryly)* Indeed I did not.

ATHELNEY-J.   And that's why I'm here and you're there.

ATHELNEY-JONES moves to the entrance and calls out:

     (Calling off) Constable?

CONSTABLE   *(Off)* Sir?

ATHELNEY-J.   *(Calling off)* Ask Mr. Sholto to step this way.

WATSON   *(To HOLMES; quietly)* He's not about to – *(do what I think)*

HOLMES   *(To WATSON; quietly)* I didn't think he'd take it this far, but I rather fear he is.

84

The CONSTABLE enters sheepishly.

CONSTABLE   He's down the gardens with the Miss.

ATHELNEY-J.   Down the...? Say that again. Go on. Say it again.

A beat.

CONSTABLE   He –

ATHELNEY-J.   I didn't mean it! Was my instruction to keep them in a room together at all unclear?

CONSTABLE   No sir, but...

ATHELNEY-J.   "No sir, but..."

CONSTABLE   Well, it's his house, sir.

ATHELNEY-J.   His house? His house? He's a murder suspect, you dolt! Come here; let me explain some fundamentals of police work to you that might not have yet reached Upper Norwood...

He moves to the exit, turning before he leaves:

        (To HOLMES & WATSON) And don't you two go anywhere either.

ATHELNEY-JONES exits with the CONSTABLE.

HOLMES   Watson, he's wrong.

WATSON   He's also drunk.

HOLMES   I need you to do something for me. If you are willing. I know it's late.

WATSON   Is it? Damn watch.

HOLMES   First, get Miss Morstan back to Lower Camberwell; she shouldn't be around this.

WATSON   Of course; then...?

HOLMES starts scribbling in his notepad.

HOLMES   Go on to No. 3 Pinchin Lane, down near the water's edge at Lambeth. Ask for Sherman. Give him your handkerchief; tell him Toby needs to get on a scent.

HOLMES hands WATSON the note.

                There.

WATSON   Now?

HOLMES   No; I may need your assistance getting through to the Inspector first.

ATHELNEY-JONES enters.

ATHELNEY-J. I swear to you, it's lucky I'm here.

HOLMES   *(To ATHELNEY-JONES)* Inspector, this is a grave mistake.

ATHELNEY-J. I thought you'd say that.

HOLMES   Think, man. It doesn't add up.

ATHELNEY-J. I am thinking, and I'll tell you something Mr. High-and-Mighty Sherlock Holmes – your interference is not welcome or wanted. Never was, never will be.

A beat.

HOLMES   For the sake of Mr. Sholto, shall we put personal grievances aside?

WATSON	Personal what?
ATHELNEY-J.	Is that what you think? You think this is about Bishopsgate, do you?
HOLMES	Isn't it?
WATSON	Bishopsgate?
HOLMES	It was a jewellery case.
ATHELNEY-J.	Oh, that's right; dismiss it like it was just another turn. *(Anger)* Bishopsgate should have made me! Instead, in comes this, this popinjay...
HOLMES	*(Amused)* Popinjay?
ATHELNEY-J.	Popinjay! Spouting his theories and, and, and his ideas...
WATSON	And his facts?
ATHELNEY-J.	Well... you can prove anything with *facts*, can't you? *(Laughing bitterly)* Poison darts. The only thing poisonous in here is you. So clever, aren't you? Inventing a profession for yourself.
WATSON	All he does is help!
ATHELNEY-J.	And did he ever consider what his "help" does to us coppers? If he's there, we're under his bloody microscope with the criminals... and now what do you think people say if he's not? "How do we know you're getting it right? Where's Mr. Holmes?"
WATSON	No-one's stopping you from doing a thorough job.

ATHELNEY-J. *(To WATSON)* I had to shake his hand. *(To HOLMES)* They made me shake your hand. Remember that? *(To WATSON)* Took a picture for the Police Gazette.

WATSON I didn't know about that.

HOLMES Private paper; small circulation. I was horribly embarrassed.

ATHELNEY-J. My wife, she... she called you... still calls you... a bloody genius. Know what I think? I think you're a menace! We do a good job. A good job. And people would see that better... without you around!

HOLMES Thaddeus Sholto is not the man you're looking for.

ATHELNEY-J. Ah, here he goes. And you're going to tell me who is, are you?

HOLMES Jonathan Small.

WATSON One of the four?

HOLMES Who else?

ATHELNEY-J. Who else who? What?

HOLMES Jonathan Small is the man you're seeking. He's poorly-educated; small, active, with his right leg off, and wearing a wooden stump, worn away upon the inner side. His left boot has a coarse, square-toed sole, with an iron band round the heel. He's middle-aged, sunburned, and has been a convict.

ATHELNEY-J. A one-legged man climbed through a hole in the roof?

HOLMES   No; he had an accomplice.

ATHELNEY-J.   An accomplice.

HOLMES   Yes; I don't know much about him yet, other
                than he's a very curious fellow. As small as a
                child, though strong, and – *(extremely agile)*

ATHELNEY-J.   A child and a cripple. That's the best you can
                do? Holmes, you're mad.

THADDEUS enters.

THADDEUS   You wanted to see me? Is everything all
                right?

A beat.

WATSON   For God's sake, man; don't do this. He's too
                weak. Taking him into custody, after all he's
                been through... you could finish him off!

ATHELNEY-J.   Mr. Sholto, I arrest you in the queen's name
                as being concerned in the death of your
                brother.

THADDEUS   I, I... I beg your pardon?

ATHELNEY-J.   It is my duty to inform you that anything you
                say will be used against you.

THADDEUS   There, now! Didn't I tell you?

HOLMES   Don't trouble yourself. I'll clear you of the
                charge.

ATHELNEY-J.   Don't promise too much, Mr. Theorist; don't
                promise too much! You may find it harder
                than you think.

MARY enters.

MARY	What's going on?
ATHELNEY-J.	Oh, for pity's – *(Calling off)* Constable!
THADDEUS	I can't stand it. I can't...
MARY	Doctor...?
WATSON	They're arresting poor Thaddeus.
MARY	For what?
THADDEUS	They think I... they think...

CONSTABLE enters.

ATHELNEY-J.	What is she doing up here?
CONSTABLE	She slipped past me, sir.
MARY	You've got the wrong man!
ATHELNEY-J.	I've heard that before.
HOLMES	Watson, get Miss Morstan out of here.
ATHELNEY-J.	Constable, do you think you might be able to manage taking four people into custody?
CONSTABLE	Sir.
MARY	Four people?
HOLMES	Inspector, what are you doing?
ATHELNEY-J.	I'm arresting the housekeeper Mrs. Bernstone...
MARY	No!
ATHELNEY-J.	...Lal Rao the manservant of the deceased...
WATSON	Come now...

ATHELNEY-J. ...the porter, Jack McMurdo...

THADDEUS Oh... oh dear God...

ATHELNEY-J. ...and this one here. Thaddeus Sholto. The ringleader.

THADDEUS No! Please... please...

The CONSTABLE takes THADDEUS by the arm. They exit.

MARY Can't you see he's sick?

ATHELNEY-J. He is. With guilt.

HOLMES Inspector, you have just made a huge mistake.

ATHELNEY-J. And I'll make sure everyone knows that's what you think as well. Dent some of that famous pride. Until next time, Mr. Theorist.

ATHELNEY-JONES exits. MARY is upset. WATSON takes her hand.

HOLMES *(To Watson)* Are you willing to do as I asked?

WATSON I am.

HOLMES Then go without delay; there's not a moment to lose.

MARY What do you intend to do?

HOLMES The only thing I can. Solve the whole damn case.

A beat. Lights are closing in on him.

Watson, the game is afoot!

Music swells. Lights fade. All exit. **End of Act One**

Act Two.

Music plays. The stage has been reset during the interval. The two sets of tables are places base-to-base, one on top of the other, so as to resemble cages. They, along with two of the columns, are positioned stage left. WATSON and MARY enter.

MARY   This looks like the place.

WATSON   *(To audience)* Said Mary, walking cautiously among the animal cages in the yard at number three, Pinchin Lane.

MARY   Should we knock?

WATSON   *(To audience)* It was late, and the early evening chill had turned into a crisp night; frost in the air carried by icy breaths of wind.

MARY   *(Calling)* Hello?

WATSON   *(To audience)* I hadn't intended on disobeying Holmes – the cab had been en route to lower Camberwell when Miss Morstan insisted on accompanying me to Lambeth. I tried to discourage it...

MARY   This isn't a place I'd want to be on my own.

WATSON   *(To audience)* I didn't try very hard.

MARY   I'm glad you're here, Dr. Watson.

WATSON   I'm glad too. That you're here, I mean. With me. Not – *with* me, but...

MARY   What's the name of this chap?

WATSON   Ah. Er... *(Reading from note)* Sherman.

MARY   *(Calling)* Mr. Sherman?

At this the members of the company upstage all bark loudly, causing MARY and WATSON to jump.

SHERMAN *(Off)* Cut it out, you bloody idiot! D'you know what time it is?

WATSON Not really. Damn watch...

SHERMAN appears from an elevated position, peering through a gap in the set.

SHERMAN Get on with you, else I'll set forty-three dogs on you.

WATSON If you'll let one out it's just what we've come for.

SHERMAN Go on! I've got a viper up here in a bag –

WATSON A viper?

SHERMAN Bloody big one, too. I'll drop it on your head if you don't hook it.

MARY He's going to drop a snake?

WATSON Don't worry Miss Morstan. It's a bluff.

There is the hiss of a snake. A beat.

Probably. Probably a bluff.

Another hiss.

MARY God save us!

SHERMAN You got a woman down there with you?

MARY I can speak for myself, thank you.

SHERMAN I won't have my yards used for sordid business.

MARY   Sordid…?

SHERMAN   Sordid! I won't have it. Gives the dogs ideas. Now clear off!

WATSON   But we want a dog.

SHERMAN   I won't be argued with! Now stand clear, for when I say 'three,' down goes the viper.

MARY   No; please, you don't understand…

SHERMAN   One…

WATSON   I'm not here to cause trouble, I'm here on behalf of –

SHERMAN   …two…

WATSON   Mr. Sherlock Holmes has sent me.

A beat. SHERMAN stops his count.

SHERMAN   You should have said that first. Wait there, the pair of you.

He disappears from the window. Music. WATSON and MARY shiver in the early morning air. SHERMAN reappears, wiping his hands on a cloth.

A friend of Mr. Sherlock is always welcome. You mustn't mind my bein' just a wee bit short wi' you at first. The children round about are savages; there's many a one comes down this lane playing chappie. And excuse my tone, Miss – I couldn't tell in the dark that you was a lady.

He offers his hand to MARY, who takes it.

MARY   There's nothing to excuse.

94

SHERMAN	Now, what was it that Mr. Sherlock wanted, sir?
WATSON	He wanted a particular dog of yours.
SHERMAN	Ah! That'd be Toby.
MARY	Toby; that's right.
SHERMAN	You got something for him, have you?

WATSON fishes out his handkerchief.

WATSON	Here.
SHERMAN	Oh, aye. That's a stink. He'll get on that all right. Track that to the world's end, he will. You handled trackers before?
WATSON	No; er...
SHERMAN	Yeah; didn't think so. And I don't suppose you have, Miss.

MARY shakes her head politely.

	Right; well... you need to take him back to the start, let go and keep up. Mind, it could be miles.
WATSON	I should be all right.
SHERMAN	With that leg?
WATSON	Well... how fast does he run?
SHERMAN	Depends.
WATSON	On what?
SHERMAN	How old the trail is; how strong the smell. Something like what's on there...

SHERMAN looks him up and down.

Tell you what. Wait there.

WATSON   Where are you going?

SHERMAN   To get Toby, and my coat. I'll come with you. *(To MARY)* If I'm not intruding...

MARY and WATSON look at one another briefly; both amused and a touch embarrassed.

MARY   Not at all.

WATSON   I really don't want to put you to any trouble...

SHERMAN   'S all right; my wife can feed the rest of 'em if I'm gone a day. Be a tonic to see Mr. Sherlock too.

WATSON   But... how will you...? I mean...

SHERMAN   Don't worry. I done this before. I'll get Toby on *this* scent, Mr. Sherlock gets Wiggins on *my* scent, and before you know where you are whatever it is you're looking for's been found. try to keep warm. I'll be back in a twinkling!

SHERMAN exits. WATSON turns to the audience.

WATSON   *(To audience)* Incredible, the effect Holmes' name had on people from all walks of life. Wiggins and his band of Baker Street Irregulars were no different. A dozen or so urchins who all, for a shilling a day, worked miracles for the man – spying, surveilling, keeping grubby ears to the ground.

Offstage we hear a dog barking, and SHERMAN says:

SHERMAN   *(Off)* Come on then, Toby. Mr. Sherlock
                wants us.

MARY   Where to now? Back to Upper Norwood?

WATSON   For Sherman, Toby and I, yes; first we'll take
                you to your place of residence.

MARY   Dr. Watson, I – *(would rather stay on this)*

WATSON   I'm afraid I have to insist, Miss Morstan.

A beat. MARY looks at him.

                It's not because I... ah, that is... I'm...
                concerned for your standing with your
                employers. A governess returning home late is
                better than one not returning at all.

MARY   Yes; yes, I see. Of course.

They smile at one another.

                Thank you for allowing me to accompany
                you.

WATSON   Think nothing of it.

A beat.

MARY   This has been a most awful business.

WATSON   Mmm.

MARY   And you and Mr. Holmes; this is what...?
                (you do)

WATSON   Most of the time, yes.

MARY   I don't know how you find the stomach for it.
                Poor Bartholomew. Thaddeus told me they'd
                been close as children; then...

WATSON smiles sympathetically.

> What will happen to him? To Thaddeus, I mean.

WATSON   There's no evidence against him. Don't worry.

A beat.

> I am so, so sorry about your father.

MARY   Thank you, Dr. Watson.

WATSON   John; please.

MARY   John. Of course. And you must call me Mary.

A beat. MARY dissolves slowly into tears.

WATSON   Oh!

MARY   Forgive me...

WATSON   There's nothing to forgive. You've been through so much...

MARY   It's awful. All of it!

She reaches for his hand. He takes it. She sobs quietly, then says:

> I'm... sorry about this... I just feel... you're the only person that... I...

She fights more tears.

> Will you promise to return when you have news?

WATSON   Yes. And Holmes and I will deliver your fortune to you.

MARY   I don't doubt it.

SHERMAN   *(Off)* May I join you yet or are you still billing and cooing?

MARY and WATSON look at one another, embarrassed again. Music. With a further squeeze of his hand, MARY exits.

WATSON   *(To audience)* Less than five minutes after Sherman and I arrived at Pondicherry Lodge, Toby was off, face to the ground, tail wagging happily, with Sherman in hot pursuit. I returned to Baker Street, to a hot bath and a good night's sleep. I woke to a note from Holmes:

HOLMES   *(Off)* Watson – Toby and Wiggins came through. As soon as you can, meet me at the wharf at the end of Broad Street. And from now on, I suggest you keep your revolver close at hand. Sincerely. H.

WATSON   Here we go again...

Music. A routine. The stage is reconfigured; the tables now arranged together to form our wharf; a catwalk-like structure. Hung onto one of the columns is a weather-worn sign reading "Mordecai Smith Boat Hire;" on another, a life ring. HOLMES and WATSON enter and take up positions close to the sign.

                  Toby followed the scent all the way here?

HOLMES   By way of a creosote barrel, according to Sherman. Almost threw him off. I did say he was good.

WATSON   How did you make such an acquaintance?

HOLMES   Oh, I did him a small service years ago. A trifle, really.

WATSON   You made him a trifle?

99

HOLMES	Very droll.
WATSON	Do you know he keeps a viper in a bag?
HOLMES	I didn't, but it doesn't surprise me.
WATSON	So? Where to next?
HOLMES	This, Watson, is where the trail goes cold. It would appear that they took to water here, and I believe Mordecai Smith to be the man who took them. I've been hammering on his door to no avail; as you arrived I dispatched one of the Irregulars to fetch his wife.
WATSON	Then since we have a moment, perhaps you could explain how you came to know so much about our quarry. The facts you gave Athelney-Jones last night –
HOLMES	Ah, yes. Poor, deluded Jones. I had to suffer more of his sarcasms after you left. He returned seeking confirmations of his ludicrous version of events.
WATSON	Is it any more ludicrous than ours?
HOLMES	Other than the fact that ours happens to be true, no. But the explanation is simplicity itself.
WATSON	To you, perhaps.
HOLMES	Here, then, is the case in a nutshell: Two officers in command of a convict-guard –
WATSON	Morstan and Sholto.
HOLMES	– learn an important secret as to buried treasure. A map is drawn for them by an

Englishman named Jonathan Small, signed on behalf of himself and his associates.

WATSON   Ah! The so-called "Sign of four."

HOLMES   The same. Now, aided by this chart, Major Sholto gets the treasure and brings it to England, leaving the others empty-handed.

WATSON   But why did Jonathan Small not get the treasure himself?

HOLMES   The answer is obvious.

WATSON   I do wish you'd stop saying things like that.

HOLMES   The chart is dated at a time when Morstan was brought into close association with convicts. Jonathan Small didn't get the treasure because he and his associates were themselves convicts and couldn't get away.

WATSON   That's speculation at best.

HOLMES   Is it? Let's see how it fits with the rest of the story. Major Sholto remains at peace for some years, the treasure safely in his possession. Then he receives a letter from India which gives him a great fright.

WATSON   Because the men he'd wronged had been released.

HOLMES   Escaped is more likely – he'd have known their term of imprisonment.

WATSON   Yes... yes!

HOLMES   So he guards himself against a wooden-legged man. A white man, mark you, for he mistakes a white tradesman for him, and actually fires a pistol at him.

WATSON   And because there was only one Englishman's name on the chart…

HOLMES   …we can confidently say that the wooden-legged man is Jonathan Small. Now, put yourself in Small's place. He comes to England with two notions:

WATSON   Taking back what's his?

HOLMES   And revenge. The face at the window tells us he found out where Sholto lived – I suspect someone on the inside tipped him off – but what he couldn't find out was the location of the treasure.

WATSON   Because only the Major knew. Oh; and the servant, Lal…

HOLMES   Chowdar, though he's dead by this point.

WATSON   Of course; sorry.

HOLMES   Suddenly Small learns that the major is on his death-bed. Terrified that the secret of the treasure will die with him, he sneaks past the guards and makes his way to the dying man's window –

WATSON   Where he is seen.

HOLMES   Later that night he enters the room, searching for some clue relating to the treasure, and finally leaving a memento of his visit in the short inscription upon the card. This last I suspect he'd planned to leave – probably after murdering the Major with his own hands. Do you follow all this?

WATSON   Very clearly.

HOLMES   Good. Now we come forward to more recent events. Small must have kept watch on the property, but how often is harder to say. Then comes Bartholomew's discovery, and he's instantly informed of it.

WATSON   The inside man again.

HOLMES   With his wooden leg, Small is utterly unable to reach the lofty room alone. He takes with him, however, a rather curious associate, who gets over this difficulty, but dips his foot into creosote, whence comes Toby, and a six-mile run for our Mr. Sherman.

WATSON   But it was the associate who killed Bartholomew.

HOLMES   Quite so. And judging by the way Small stamped about when he got into the room, it was much against his wishes. The theft worked much as I explained it before. As to his personal appearance he must be middle-aged, and must be sunburned after serving his time in the Andamans. His height is readily calculated from the length of his stride, and we know his face from the description given to us by poor Thaddeus. I don't know that there is anything else.

A beat. HOLMES paces.

Where the blazes is this woman? The trail grows colder by the second.

WATSON   Perhaps she's absconded too.

HOLMES   I don't think they're involved. At least not directly. Did you remember your pistol?

WATSON   Yes, I took it from the...

WATSON reaches for where he would normally conceal his revolver. It's not there.

        I could have sworn...

HOLMES   Pay it no mind. You have your stick at least. It's possible we may need something of the sort if we get to their lair.

HOLMES removes his own revolver, breaks it, examines the chamber and replaces it while saying:

        Jonathan I leave to you, but if the other turns nasty I shall shoot him dead.

At this a woman, MRS. SMITH, enters.

MRS. SMITH   Are you him what the street Arab fetched me for?

HOLMES puts the revolver away and turns.

        Only I needed to find someone to watch the little 'uns.

HOLMES   You have children, Mrs. Smith?

MRS. SMITH   Twelve.

HOLMES   Twelve! Bless my soul!

MRS. SMITH   Bless mine an' all while you're at it. They're a lot to handle, 'specially when my man's away.

HOLMES   Away, is he? That's a shame.

MRS. SMITH   Since yesterday morning. Truth be told I'm starting to get worried, but... if it was about a boat, sir, maybe I could serve as well.

HOLMES   Ah, yes; I wanted to hire his steam launch.

MRS. SMITH   Wouldn't you know; that's what he's gone off in! That's what puzzles me; for I know there ain't more coals in her than would take her to about Woolwich and back.

HOLMES   He might have bought some at a wharf down the river.

MRS. SMITH   With what they charge? No fear. And he didn't have time for no haggling, what with that man forever breathing down his neck and wanting to be off.

HOLMES   A man, you say?

MRS. SMITH   Oh yeah. Brown as a berry he is. Called more'n once for my old man. It was him as roused him up last night.

HOLMES   My dear Mrs. Smith. How could you possibly tell that it was the same man who came in the night?

MRS. SMITH   I could hear his wooden leg clackin' on the stones, that's how.

WATSON is about to explode with delight that they are on the right track but HOLMES stops him, and calmly says:

HOLMES   And was he alone, this wooden-legged man?

MRS. SMITH   Didn't hear no-one else; just him, my man and our eldest, Jim. But oooh, I don't like him sir; really I don't.

HOLMES	No, I see that. Shame; I wanted a steam launch, and I've heard good reports of the – oh, what's the name…?
MRS. SMITH	The *Aurora*, sir.
HOLMES	Ah! She's not that old green launch with a yellow line, very broad in the beam?
MRS. SMITH	No, indeed. She's as trim a little thing as any on the river. She's been fresh painted, black with two red streaks.
HOLMES	Thanks. I'm sure you're worrying about nothing. I expect Mr. Smith will be waiting for you when you get home.
MRS. SMITH	I'll have a word or two to say to him if he is; making me fretful.
HOLMES	Indeed. I'll tell you what – I'm going down the river today. If I see anything of the *Aurora* I'll let him know you're uneasy. A black funnel, you say?
MRS. SMITH	Black with a white band.
HOLMES	Of course. It was the sides which were black. Good-morning, Mrs. Smith – I'll let you get back to your children, and… here; here's half a crown for your troubles.
MRS. SMITH	Bless you, sir. You're a gent.

MRS. SMITH exits.

WATSON	Holmes, what the Devil…?
HOLMES	The trick with people of that sort is never to let them think their information is important. If you do, they'll shut up like an oyster. Now

106

we have the name and description of the craft.
I'll need to have another word with Wiggins.

WATSON   Surely not. We could hire a launch; search upriver.

HOLMES   Alone? It'd take days. There are hundreds of landing points between here and Greenwich.

WATSON   What then? The Police?

HOLMES   Athelney-Jones? A last resort. The game is ours, Watson.

WATSON   Then we put the word out up the river.

HOLMES   We do that and they get wind of it, we'll lose them, and the treasure, forever. No; we need them to think that there is no suspicion on them at all. Our dear Inspector should help with that.

WATSON   Should he?

HOLMES   If he hasn't already. We'll pick up a city final on the way back to Baker Street and find out. But first, Wiggins. The groundwork is laid. We have only to wait...

Music. The space is reconfigured, recreating Baker Street as we saw it at the start of the play. WATSON sits in the chair by the table reading a newspaper. HOLMES stands by the window, violin in hand. He plucks at the strings as WATSON reads.

WATSON   *(Reading)* "About twelve o'clock last night Mr. Bartholomew Sholto, of Pondicherry Lodge, Upper Norwood, was found dead in his room under circumstances which point to foul play. No actual traces of violence were found upon Mr. Sholto's person, but a valuable collection of Indian gems which the deceased gentleman had inherited from his father has been carried off."

HOLMES   *(Breaking off)* Read on. It gets better.

WATSON   *(Reading)* "The discovery was first made by Mr. Sherlock Holmes and Dr. Watson," – at least they got my name right – "who had called at the house with Mr. Thaddeus Sholto, brother of the deceased.

HOLMES puts down the violin.

HOLMES   Here it comes…

WATSON   *(Reading)* "By a singular piece of good fortune, Mr. Athelney Jones, the well-known member of the detective police force, happened to be at the Norwood Police Station. His trained and experienced faculties were at once directed towards the detection of the criminals, with the gratifying result that the brother, Thaddeus Sholto, has already been arrested, together with the housekeeper, Mrs. Bernstone, an Indian butler named Lal Rao, and a porter, or gatekeeper, the former prize-fighter Jack McMurdo."

HOLMES   What do you think of it?

WATSON   *(Reading)* "It is quite certain that the thief…" mm-hmm… "…for Mr. Jones's well-known technical knowledge and his powers of minute observation have enabled him to prove conclusively that this quartet of miscreants…"

A beat.

108

HOLMES   Isn't it wonderful?

WATSON   I despair.

HOLMES   It serves our purpose perfectly. Small will read this and think he's in the clear. He'll be out on the water and we'll have him.

HOLMES looks at WATSON.

               Take a nap; you look tired.

WATSON   I'm sorry?

HOLMES   Aren't you?

WATSON   Exhausted. Aren't you?

HOLMES   You know me; when I'm engaged with a problem such as this I rarely sleep. Of course, come the conclusion I'll be limp as a rag for a week, but now there's much to learn.

WATSON   I thought you said we were just waiting.

HOLMES   Ah, but *while* we wait…

HOLMES collects a book from a shelf.

               For instance, did you know that the Andaman Islands are home to the smallest race of humans upon the earth?

WATSON   When did you learn that?

HOLMES   As you took your bath.

WATSON   Of course you did. I don't know why I'm surprised.

HOLMES   Cannibals, according to the text. And their preferred weapon, aside from the bow…?

WATSON   Poison darts?

HOLMES   Precisely.

WATSON   I can imagine what Athelney-Jones would say to that.

HOLMES   *'Wir sind gewohnt daß die Menschen verhöhnen was sie nicht verstehen.'* Goethe is always pithy. Come, Watson. Close your eyes. I'll play a while; soothe you to your rest...

HOLMES takes up his violin.

WATSON   You really... you really don't have to...

HOLMES   Practice in all things, Watson. Practice in all things...

WATSON closes his eyes and HOLMES begins to play. The sounds he produces are not good. At all. WATSON talks to the audience.

WATSON   *(To audience)* In the years following I can surely tell you that Holmes' playing did improve... as a learner, however, he did not produce sounds that would induce sleep in anyone. Including the deaf.

HOLMES stops playing and exits. Music continues as WATSON talks.

That first day, Holmes was full of patience and high hopes of a swift resolution. His mood was up and we sat chatting amiably. About the case, yes; but also about his methods, and London... and Mary. I visited her with an update as promised... but still kept my feelings to myself. It sent a little thrill of joy to my heart to notice that she showed no sign of elation at the prospect of riches.

The music starts to change, taking on a more brooding tone.

Three fruitless days followed. Reports from Wiggins and his team were not encouraging. No sightings of the *Aurora* either up or down river. Holmes placed an advertisement in the Standard appealing for information on a missing father and son and their steam launch. Nothing.

The music gets more spiky and atonal.

The mood at Baker Street darkened. We all felt it. Holmes stamped about the place in a brown study, moving listlessly from room to room and casting lengthening glances at the needle. He did not partake.

The music changes again; darkening.

It was his practice, when frustrated by a case, that he would set himself another challenge to keep his mind in the best of order. So it was that he started experimenting with acidic and alkaline compounds so noxious that both Mrs. Hudson and I were forced to take a walk in the rain for fear of passing out.

The music starts to calm a little.

On the fifth day I descended to the study to find no odours from the room upstairs, no violining... and no Holmes. A note demanding I stay for word of a sighting was the only clue that he was out. But it wasn't

111

Wiggins who visited that afternoon. It was a far more unlikely guest...

HUDSON enters. Lights.

HUDSON   There's a Policeman downstairs.

WATSON   Oh?

HUDSON   Says he's looking for Mr. Holmes... or a Dr. Wilson...

A beat.

Shall I send him up, or send him packing?

WATSON   Send him up.

HUDSON   Very good.

WATSON   Oh; Mrs. Hudson?

HUDSON   Yes sir?

WATSON   Did Holmes mention anything about where he was headed?

HUDSON   No, but by the way he was dressed...

WATSON   How was that?

HUDSON   Like a sailor. Pea-jacket; coarse red scarf round his neck. Didn't suit him.

WATSON   Perhaps he's not the man for undercover work.

HUDSON   Well... better him than you.

WATSON   What does that mean?

HUDSON   *(Smiling)* Don't ask me. Ask the spotted dog.

112

WATSON   That will be all, Mrs. Hudson.

HUDSON   Very good, sir.

HUDSON exits, and after a moment or two, ATHELNEY-JONES, cutting a decidedly less confident (but more sober) figure than last we saw him, enters.

WATSON   Inspector Jones.

ATHELNEY-J.   Doctor Watson.

WATSON   Mrs. Hudson's doing?

ATHELNEY-JONES nods.

            Well. Would you like to sit?

ATHELNEY-J.   In a moment sir. First, I'd – my behaviour the other night; first to last, it was... I let myself down, sir.

WATSON   I wouldn't say that.

ATHELNEY-J.   You would, sir. And I know Mr. Holmes would.

WATSON   No, he'd let you know he was thinking it.

ATHELNEY-JONES takes a moment to think about this.

ATHELNEY-J.   Yes. Yes, you're probably right; he would, sir.

He sits.

            I was wrong.

WATSON   We've been over this.

ATHELNEY-J.   About the case at Upper Norwood. We've released Mr. Sholto and the housekeeper, Mrs. Bernstone. It's been in the papers.

WATSON   I saw, yes.

ATHELNEY-J. Turns out they both had alibis.

WATSON   It happens. Drink? Whiskey and soda, isn't it?

ATHELNEY-J. How did...?

A beat.

Er... yes; just a small one.

WATSON goes to get drinks.

Mr. Holmes, he. He does have a unique, er... and, unconventional, er...

WATSON   Indeed.

ATHELNEY-J. But he's... and I'll go on record as saying this... he's a fine detective. Perhaps the best of them.

WATSON   Better than you?

WATSON hands ATHELNEY-JONES his drink.

Apologies. That was uncalled for.

ATHELNEY-JONES waves away the apology and takes a sip.

Is there something I can help you with while we wait?

ATHELNEY-J. It's the waiting I'm here for.

WATSON   I don't follow.

ATHELNEY-J. He sent me a telegram today.

WATSON   *Holmes* did?

ATHELNEY-J.   *(Reading)* "Go to Baker Street at once. If I have not returned, wait for me. I am close on the track of the Sholto gang. You can come with us tonight if you want to be in at the finish."

WATSON   He must have picked up the scent again.

ATHELNEY-J.   Course, it might all come to nought, but as an officer of the law I'm duty-bound to –

HUDSON enters. An OLD MAN follows her. This is HOLMES in disguise, though no-one appears to recognise him.

HUDSON   Sorry to intrude. Another visitor to see you.

OLD MAN   It's Mr. Holmes I've come to see.

HUDSON   So you've said. Repeatedly. *(To WATSON)* Says he's got a message for him.

WATSON   Leave him with me, Mrs. Hudson.

HUDSON   Thank you, sir.

HUDSON exits. The OLD MAN watches her leave.

WATSON   I'm Dr. Watson. This is Inspector Athelney-Jones of the Yard. You can tell me any message you have for Mr. Holmes.

OLD MAN   It was to him himself I was to tell it.

WATSON   Was it about Mordecai Smith's boat?

OLD MAN   What? Oh; yes. I knows well where it is. An' I knows where the men he is after are. An' I knows where the treasure is. I knows all about everything.

WATSON   Then tell me, and I'll let him know.

OLD MAN   It was to him I was to tell it.

WATSON   You'll have to wait for him then.

OLD MAN   No, no; I ain't goin' to lose a whole day to please no one. If Mr. Holmes ain't here, then Mr. Holmes must find it all out for himself. I don't care about the look of either of you, and I won't tell a word.

He turns to leave but ATHELNEY-JONES stands in his way.

ATHELNEY-J.   Sir, if you have important information then whether you like or not you'll need to stay until Mr. Holmes returns.

WATSON   We'll recompense you for the loss of your time.

The OLD MAN shrugs, chuntering resignedly to himself.

WATSON   Another drink while we wait?

ATHELNEY-J.   I probably shouldn't, but why not?

WATSON stands and heads over to where the whiskey sits in its decanter. At once the OLD MAN has HOLMES' voice.

HOLMES   I hope you're going to offer me one of those.

WATSON   Holmes?

The OLD MAN removes the disguise, revealing the truth.

      What...?

HOLMES   I've been dressed like this all day. Seemed to me to be an adequate disguise... I'm surprised it fooled you though.

WATSON   It did.

ATHELNEY-J.   Not me. I recognised the twinkle in your eye.

HOLMES   Is that so?

A beat.

ATHELNEY-J.   No. Not really, no. You had me. You could be on the London stage.

WATSON   Where have you been?

HOLMES   I'll tell you, but we have to be on the water within the hour. Inspector, I take it I can rely on you?

ATHELNEY-J.   All arrangements are made.

HOLMES   Then let's leave. And Watson?

WATSON   Yes?

HOLMES   Get your gun.

Music. The stage is re-set; furniture arranged to create the appearance of the prow of a boat The prow goes downstage, with HOLMES and WATSON slightly upstage of it and elevated by the lower tables; ATHELNEY-JONES is in front of them, tucked into the very front. behind them. Music underscores this section, the intensity of the music initially undulating then building as the chase ramps up.

ATHELNEY-J.   Where are they?

HOLMES   Another half-mile at this speed and you'll see them sure enough.

WATSON   How did you find them?

HOLMES   It came to me while experimenting with alkaloids. The one sure-fire way of keeping a boat out of sight but ready for launch.

WATSON	What? What did we miss?
HOLMES	Repairs.
ATHELNEY-J.	Repairs?
WATSON	*(Cottoning on)* Repairs... of course...
HOLMES	After that, it was just a matter of finding which yard and sticking one of the irregulars on it.
ATHELNEY-J.	I don't think I understand.
WATSON	If Small had damaged the *Aurora* in some easily repairable way – or even if he'd wanted a modification made to the hull – he'd pay for it to be done at a yard with dry-docking.
HOLMES	Just so. The boat would be off the water, fixed and hidden, the yard awaiting payment before releasing the craft back onto the Thames.
WATSON	Small can afford it after all.
ATHELNEY-J.	I think I see her!

They all look.

HOLMES	Yes. Yes; that's the *Aurora*.
ATHELNEY-J.	Get us running at full speed, men!

He looks forward.

The chase is on.

Music. Starts to build from here.

WATSON	*(To audience)* Slipping into the Thames at Jacobson's Yard, the *Aurora* moved

gracefully; silently. Our boat, bigger in body and with more men to fire the engine, devoured the water between us.

HOLMES   Two hundred yards...

ATHELNEY-J.   Faster!

HOLMES   Hold course.

WATSON   Come on!

HOLMES   Pile it on, men! Pile it on!

ATHELNEY-J.   I doubt we'll catch her.

HOLMES   We must!

WATSON   *(To audience)* The furnace of our boat throbbed as if alive; engines clanking and whirring.

HOLMES   One hundred and seventy!

ATHELNEY-J.   Faster!

WATSON   *(To audience)* Our prow cut through the river-water and sent two rolling waves to right and to left of us. With every thump of the engines we sprang and quivered like a living thing.

HOLMES   One-forty!

ATHELNEY-J.   Come on!

HOLMES   Keep it up! Get every pound of steam you can!

WATSON   *(To audience)* We flashed past barges, steamers, merchant-vessels, in and out, behind this one and round the other. The

119

Aurora thundered on, and still we followed close upon her track.

HOLMES   One hundred!

WATSON   Eighty!

ATHELNEY-J. Seventy!

HOLMES   That's it, boys! We'll have her yet!

There is the sound of a boat's horn and everyone looks to the right.

ATHELNEY-J. Watch out!

WATSON   *(To audience)* A tug with three barges in tow blundered in between us.

ATHELNEY-J. Hard down helm!

WATSON   Jesus!

HOLMES   All ahead flank! Right full rudder!

ATHELNEY-J. Turn, damn you! Turn!

WATSON   We're done for!

ATHELNEY-J. Brace for impact!

There is the sound of a boat's horn, louder than ever.

WATSON   *(To audience)* How we avoided a collision I'll never know. The margin between us could have been measured in inches.

ATHELNEY-J. We've lost her. Damn it!

HOLMES   Never!

WATSON   How far, Holmes?

HOLMES   Two hundred and forty yards.

ATHELNEY-J. Come on!

HOLMES We've caught her once; let's do it again!

WATSON *(To audience)* Our course corrected, we shot through the Pool, past the West India Docks, down the long Deptford Reach, and up again after rounding the Isle of Dogs. Our boilers were strained to their utmost, and the frail shell vibrated and creaked with the fierce energy which was driving us along.

ATHELNEY-J. We're closing again.

HOLMES No mistakes this time, men – they know we're onto them!

ATHELNEY-J. There's a boy at the tiller!

HOLMES That'll be Smith's son, Jim. Neither he nor his father are to be harmed. Agreed?

ATHELNEY-J. It'll be a long time until I disagree with you again.

WATSON *(To audience)* We could see one man sat by the stern, with something black between his knees over which he stooped. Beside him lay a dark mass which looked like a Newfoundland dog.

HOLMES Stay in their slipstream. Watch every turn.

ATHELNEY-J. You'll not lose us a second time.

HOLMES One hundred and fifty yards.

WATSON *(To audience)* At Greenwich we were about one hundred and twenty paces behind them. At Blackwall we couldn't have been more than eighty.

HOLMES   See by their furnace. Smith's tiring! There's only him to work it!

ATHELNEY-J.   Pile it on, boys!

HOLMES   Sixty yards! Fifty!

WATSON   *(To audience)* The man in the stern still crouched upon the deck, and his arms were moving as though he were busy, while every now and then he would look up and measure with a glance the distance which still separated us.

ATHELNEY-J.   What's he doing? Losing ballast?

WATSON   Whatever it is, the game's up. He must know that!

HOLMES   Forty yards! Thirty!

WATSON   *(To audience)* By the time we reached Barking Level and Plumstead Marshes we were not more than four boat's lengths behind them, both vessels flying at a tremendous pace.

HOLMES   All yours, Inspector Jones.

ATHELNEY-J.   Really?

Puffed up with pride and gratitude, ATHELNEY-JONES cries:

        Stop! Stop in the name of the law!

WATSON   *(To audience)* At our hail the man in the stern cursed us, springing up, shaking his fists... and revealing the wooden stump where his right leg ought to have been.

HOLMES draws his pistol.

HOLMES Watson...

WATSON *(To audience)* There was movement in the bundle upon the deck. It straightened itself into the smallest man I have ever seen with a great, misshapen head and a shock of tangled, dishevelled hair.

ATHELNEY-J. My God, what is that thing?

WATSON The accomplice...

HOLMES Watson...

WATSON *(To audience)* He was wrapped in a blanket, which left only his face exposed; but that face was enough to give even the bravest man a sleepless night. Never have I seen features so deeply marked with cruelty.

HOLMES Watson!

WATSON *(To audience)* His eyes glowed, and his lips were writhed back from his teeth, which grinned at us with a half animal fury. I was frozen at the sight, until –

HOLMES Watson! Your revolver!

WATSON draws his pistol.

(Calmly) Fire only if he raises his hand.

ATHELNEY-J. The game's up, Small. Constable, fetch the gaff hooks; let's draw them in.

WATSON *(To audience)* I can see the two of them now as they stood, Small shrieking out curses, and the unhallowed dwarf with his strong yellow teeth gnashing at us in the light of our lantern. I suspect that sight will live with me to my dying day... mostly because of what happened next.

ATHELNEY-J.   Mr. Smith; young Jim... bring the boat to shore. You have nothing to fear from us.

ATHELNEY-JONES sees movement from the little man.

Stand still. Still, I say!

HOLMES   Watson...

WATSON   Jones; down!

ATHELNEY-J.   No...!

Slow-motion. In the score is mixed the sound of a blow-pipe, fired just as HOLMES and WATSON raise and discharge their pistols. The guns, whether created live by the musicians or pre-recorded and played over the top, should sound like cannons. The large explosive sound ought to switch us from live to recorded sound. HOLMES and WATSON hold their freeze as the remaining members of the company enter and disassemble the boat around them. ATHELNEY-JONES exits. HOLMES' voice is heard as he and WATSON exit and SMALL enters the space. He sits and shifts uncomfortably in his chair.

HOLMES   *(Off)* Jonathan Small... you gave us all quite a chase. You will know that we recovered the treasure chest from the *Aurora*, and that Inspector Athelney-Jones is waiting for you downstairs, and yet – call it an indulgence if you will, but I have been granted a moment or two to discover the truth of all this. So... before you are taken away... do you want to tell us how it all started?

Lights open up to incorporate the rest of the stage. Though ostensibly he is talking to HOLMES, he addresses the audience for the most part.

124

SMALL   *(To audience)* I'm a Lancashire man. Born in Blackburn. Large family. No real prospects, so I... joined the army; came to India. I could tell you I wanted to return home a hero, get my mother out of debt – in truth I just wanted to get by.

A beat

Wasn't in the army long. Crocodile took my leg when I was swimming in the Ganges. Hadn't been for my company Sergeant, John Hodder, he'd have had the rest of me too. So. There I was, a useless cripple of eighteen. No good for the army. No good at home, 'cept... more rain there, so I stayed.

A beat.

Fellow named Abelwhite took me on. Friend of our Colonel's. Plantation owner; needed an overseer up in Muttra, near the border of the North West provinces. Long story short, the Colonel recommended me, and since most of what I was doing was on horseback... I was hired. And that's where I met the best friend I'll ever have. Dost Akbar.

AKBAR enters.

See, what you need to understand is, we've got it wrong. Us British. We call them savages; they're not savages. We're the savages. Their life is all about peace, and harmony, and love and prayer. Us? We're like – we're bloody locusts. Take everything from them, sell them bits of it back and whip them if they don't say thank you.

AKBAR Thank you.

SMALL What's that?

AKBAR Thank you, Sahib.

SMALL For what?

AKBAR The other overseers, they beat; curse... deny us water. You are not like that.

SMALL Well... not the decent thing to do, is it?

AKBAR How much of this is decent?

A beat.

SMALL Not much, to be honest.

AKBAR No.

AKBAR puts his hand out to SMALL.

I am Dost Akbar.

SMALL Jonathan Small.

AKBAR Thank you, Jonathan Small. In all of this, I am glad to know you.

AKBAR turns to leave.

SMALL Your, ah... your English is very good.

AKBAR Huh?

SMALL *(Points)* You. Good English.

AKBAR *(Smiling)* You. Bad English.

He waves and exits.

SMALL　　　　*(To audience)* The things I learned from that man... patience; forgiveness... acceptance. Even came to accept the old peg-leg in time. Course, when reports got back that I wasn't as hard on the workers, old Abelwhite came down hard on me. I expected it. He was playing his role. I could see in his eyes he knew I was right, but... the East India Company rule with an iron fist, so...

JOANNA DAWSON enters with a glass of lemonade for SMALL.

JOANNA　　　Jonathan?

SMALL　　　　*(To audience)* The other overseers were the same. I'm sure they all wanted to be like me. I'd like to think that, anyway. Joanna, for instance – wife of a mate of mine; Peter Dawson; she understood.

JOANNA　　　Here.

SMALL　　　　Thanks.

He doesn't drink it.

JOANNA　　　You could at least *pretend* to drink some.

SMALL　　　　Oh, it's not that I don't like it; just...

JOANNA　　　...your friend likes it more than you. I know.

SMALL　　　　His recipe.

JOANNA　　　Which I perfected.

SMALL　　　　That you did.

JOANNA　　　All right. Take him a glass.

SMALL   Actually…

AKBAR enters.

JOANNA   Oh! Er…

AKBAR   The mint is a delicious addition, Miss.

JOANNA   Thank you. *(To SMALL)* Did you teach him to say that?

SMALL shakes his head.

(To AKBAR) You speak English very well. Were you a school teacher?

AKBAR   No… but I wasn't always a slave.

JOANNA   Ah. I see. It must be… hard.

AKBAR   Living and dying without understanding your purpose is harder.

A beat.

JOANNA   Right. Yes; well…

AKBAR   I didn't mean to embarrass you.

JOANNA   No, of course. You didn't. Just… ah…

A beat.

Think I might, ah… take the shade.

She takes the lemonade over to AKBAR. Hands him the glass. He drinks it in one.

Any time you want more, you let me know.

AKBAR nods and smiles. He exits. JOANNA watches him go.

He's exceptional.

SMALL   He is... and he isn't.

She looks at him and exits.

(To audience) You could say I knew it was coming, but I didn't. People over there, they... well, they bond together; like they're against a common enemy... not realising it's the wrong one. Abelwhite; Dawson... didn't get it. What's right and what's wrong.

We hear the sound of conflict; of bloodshed and slaughter.

Then came the uprising.

Screams, seemingly from everywhere. Everyone offstage yelling, screaming. Yelling on the soundtrack, the sounds of burning.

Then he got it. And so did everyone else.

JOANNA enters; her shirt torn and covered in blood.

Joanna?

JOANNA   They're... they're here. Get on your horse. Ride. Ride while you still... can... just... ride...

SMALL   Good God. Where's – ?

JOANNA   Peter's... dead... I... he...

She collapses into his arms. AKBAR enters.

AKBAR   Jonathan!

SMALL   Are... are you part of this?

AKBAR   No. Yes. I don't know.

Shouts from close by. AKBAR draws a dagger.

Lie down.

SMALL   What are you doing?

AKBAR   Saving your life.

Using the dagger, he rips a hole in SMALL's shirt. He then wipes some of the blood from JOANNA's body onto his friend.

Lie on your face. Lie down!

SMALL does so. AKBAR stands, then yells in Hindi:

Kill the oppressors! Let us take back what's ours! Butcher the butchers. Freedom for India!

He turns back to SMALL.

Lie still. Goodbye, my friend.

Music. The stage is reconfigured around SMALL. AKBAR exits, as does the actor playing JOANNA. Agra fort is created. Once done, and with the stage clear, SMALL stands.

SMALL   *(To audience)* An hour later, cramped, drenched with sweat and sick to my stomach, I got up, found a horse and rode hard for Agra, where the nearest British troops were. I understood, you know? Why would they assume I was any different to any of the others?

A beat.

I reached Agra and – well, it's a savage place. Hard to defend; especially with so few men. Commanding Officer decided to take up at the Fort over the river. Bloody labyrinth, it is; rooms, passages, tunnels, sub-tunnels... anyway, they made me join the volunteer

130

corps, didn't they? The fighting went on; whole country was up like a swarm of bees. At Agra, as well as the volunteer corps, there were the 3rd Bengal Fusiliers, some Sikhs, two troops of horse, and a battery of artillery, so... not much. I was put on an outer door. Just me, all on my lonesome. Most of the time...

Lights. Another soldier, THOMAS, approaches with a wooden foot-stool.

THOMAS   Evening, Small.

SMALL   Corporal Thomas.

THOMAS   Another quiet night.

SMALL   That it is.

THOMAS   Here; brought you this.

SMALL   What's that for?

THOMAS   You sit on it.

SMALL   No, I mean... why me?

THOMAS   Shahgunge.

SMALL   What's that?

THOMAS   When we went out to meet the rebels at Shahgunge in May, you fought well, so...

SMALL   That was months ago.

THOMAS   I can take it away...

SMALL   No, no. It's fine.

A beat.

THOMAS   Are you going to sit on it?

SMALL   Eventually, yes. Takes me a little while to get down, that's all.

THOMAS   Right. Well. Merry Christmas, Small.

He turns and exits. SMALL calls after him:

SMALL   That was months ago as well!

There's no reply. SMALL eases himself down onto the stool and is just letting out a smile of satisfaction when there is a snapping noise. SMALL stands again, picks up his rifle and looks about him.

Who goes there?

Nothing.

Hello?

Nothing.

Look, I am going to sit on it. I was doing; then I heard something, and...

A Sikh soldier enters. This is Abdullah KHAN. He nods at SMALL.

Oh. Evening. You my relief?

KHAN shakes his head.

Only I could do with... you know...

SMALL needs the toilet. KHAN nods silently, suggesting he relieve himself here.

Out here? Where?

KHAN again points to a place close by. SMALL shrugs and turns away from KHAN. .

As long as you watch the door while I –

As soon as SMALL's back is to KHAN, the Sikh's knife is drawn and round SMALL's throat.

KHAN   Stay very still. I have no wish to kill you.

SMALL   I have no wish to be killed.

KHAN   Then let us understand one another. My name is Abdullah Khan; I'm part of the Sikh regiment here at Fort Agra.

SMALL   Is this part of the uprising?

KHAN   It has nothing to with that. I'm now going to raise my dagger. Don't make a sound. The Fort is safe enough.

KHAN takes the blade away and sheaths it before facing SMALL.

Three minutes.

SMALL   What's that?

KHAN   I give you three minutes to decide if you are with us, heart and soul, or you are not.

SMALL   With you for what?

KHAN says nothing.

How can I decide if I don't know… what if I'm not?

KHAN   Then your body goes into the ditch along with Corporal Thomas.

SMALL   And what had he ever done?

133

KHAN	Heard more than he should. And now you see I am serious.
SMALL	I know you are.
KHAN	Then listen well – not far from here is a Rajah who, fearing for his fortune at the hands of either the rebels or the British, is preparing to take drastic action. He has split his gold from his jewels. His gold he will sacrifice to whoever breaches his palace walls first, but his jewels... his jewels he has dispatched with a faithful bodyguard, and his trusted advisor, a British man named Hollis who is posing as a merchant. They are taking them to a safe place until the unpleasantness is over. Agra Fort is on his route.

KHAN looks at SMALL to see if he understands.

> You will not need to bloody your hands. We will do what is needed. Say you are with us and I swear upon the naked knife, and by the threefold oath which no Sikh was ever known to break, that you shall have your fair share of the loot. A quarter of the treasure shall be yours.

A beat.

> Do you understand history?

SMALL	I think so.
KHAN	And what do you understand by it?
SMALL	Well, it's... it's memorable events that have happened in the past.

KHAN	Such as this, yes? You won't forget this night. Does that make it history?
SMALL	I...
KHAN	You only missed three words. Just three. History is...?
SMALL	Memorable things that have happened in the past.
KHAN	To rich people.

A beat.

> You see? To rich people. We don't matter. Me, you, him... none of us. We are... footnotes. But with this... with this we are Kings. All I ask is that, for one night, you do what the British East India Company came here for.

SMALL looks nonplussed.

> You steal to get rich.

A beat.

> Now. Decide. The caravan draws closer.

SMALL	Yes. Of course. *(To audience)* A choice between riches or death is no choice at all.
KHAN	Good. Then stand at your post and let the Merchant pass through.
SMALL	Wait. You said a quarter.
KHAN	That is correct. You shall receive one; myself another. The third goes to my brother-in-arms, Mahomet Singh, and the fourth...

135

SMALL   Yes?

KHAN   Is to the bodyguard.

A noise makes them turn.

      Hurry. Help me get rid of Thomas' body!

KHAN exits.

SMALL   *(To audience)* Not more than an hour later the caravan arrived. The majority went to the main gate. Hollis was diverted to me.

HOLLIS enters, wearing traditional Indian garb.

      The longer I looked at him, the less I wanted a part in it all; yet... something in Khan's words struck me. I don't care about history... but I could definitely live like a king...

HOLLIS   Ah! A familiar face!

SMALL   Who goes there?

HOLLIS   No-one of note. I'm, ah... I'm a merchant, just on my way through. My, ah, my bodyguard, he... I didn't want to wait, so he said this door...

SMALL   What do you have with you?

HOLLIS   Oh, just a... chest containing... personal items. Sentimental value; you understand.

SMALL   Mementoes.

HOLLIS   That's it.

SMALL   Of the old country.

HOLLIS   That's it. Course, you know the trouble with India, don't you?

SMALL   Full of Indians?

HOLLIS   That's it.

A beat. SMALL smiles thinly.

SMALL   Pass. Friend.

HOLLIS   Thank you. Thank you.

HOLLIS exits.

SMALL   *(To audience)* Don't need to tell you what happened then, do I? He gets inside the door to find Khan and Singh, who bungle because they're evidently as nervous as I am. He rushes out and charges up to me, shouting –

HOLLIS   *(Off)* Help!

SMALL   Fear in his eyes, his heart, his beating heart.

HOLLIS   *(Off)* Save me!

SMALL   And it struck me that I could, when from behind me I heard –

The BODYGUARD enters, face covered and knife drawn.

BODYGUARD   Leave him to me.

SMALL   This is wrong.

BODYGUARD   And do you know what the trouble with India is?

SMALL looks at him. HOLLIS enters.

HOLLIS   Save... save me...

He dashes up to SMALL and grabs his arms, whereupon SMALL holds him tight...

> What are you doing?

...and turns him round into the onrushing blade of the BODYGUARD. Music. The dagger is plunged in several times. HOLLIS sags, lifeless, into SMALL's arms. The BODYGUARD uncovers his face and says:

BODYGUARD   Bad English.

It is, of course...

SMALL   Akbar!

Music. AKBAR shifts the body. SMALL continues.

> *(To audience)* It was the best and worst night of my life. My friend was alive but had just killed an innocent man, and with my help too. We rinsed off the blood, and we laughed and we cried, and the four of us counted the treasure.

A beat.

> Then... we walled him up. Hollis. Found a place in the catacombs beneath the fort; walled them both up. Him and Corporal Thomas. After that... well, we renewed our vow to stand by each other and agreed to conceal the treasure until the country was at peace again, at which time we'd divide it equally. We made a hollow in the wall, marked the place... and next day I wrote an agreement out, one for each of us. With the sign of four at the bottom. I'm proud to say that's an oath I'll never break. Next... well, I suppose it's the arrest, isn't it?

138

The stage is once more reconfigured behind SMALL as he continues to speak, the fort disassembled and an open space created. This will serve as the Andaman Islands.

Wilson took Delhi and Sir Colin relieved Lucknow and that was the rebellion all but done. Fresh troops came pouring in, and Nana Sahib made himself scarce over the frontier. We four started to think of the time when we could retrieve the treasure... when we were arrested for Hollis' murder.

A beat.

Turns out the Rajah had sent a spy after Hollis to make sure he didn't... well, didn't do what *we* did. He makes it back after the fighting ceases, tells what he knows, and next thing you know we're on the Andamans for life, and it's...

He sighs.

It's like the plantation. It's worse. Nothing's changed. My friends – my brothers – being treated like animals. Me; I'm white so I get a hut to myself in Hope Town and left to my own devices. They're chained together and forced into... I can't think about it. Power puts us at our worst. And the more we have, the worse we get. And of course, the irony is, we've all got a fortune... just sitting there, in a box in a wall.

A beat.

Few years go by. I end up working in the infirmary in Hope Town under Dr. Somerton. Nice fellow. Taught me a thing or two. At

139

night the Officers come and play cards –
nothing to do really, except gamble your
wages away. One of them... he's worse than
the rest. Losing all the time, but can't leave it
alone. Gives me an idea. Think I might put it
to him. This is my first conversation with
Major John Sholto.

Sound of shore wash. SHOLTO enters. SMALL approaches him.

SHOLTO   Small, is it?

SMALL   That's right, Major.

SHOLTO   Old Doc Somerton says you're after some
advice.

SMALL   I wanted to ask you, sir, who is the proper
person to whom hidden treasure should be
handed over? I know where half a million
worth lies you see, and I thought the best
thing would be to hand it over; maybe get my
sentence shortened.

A beat. SHOLTO can barely contain his excitement.

SHOLTO   Half a million?

SMALL   In jewels and pearls.

SHOLTO   Are you sure?

SMALL   Oh, yes sir, Just lying there. The real owner's
outlawed, see, and can't hold property, so it
belongs to the first comer.

SHOLTO   Yes; well – to government, Small. To
government.

SMALL   *(To audience)* I knew I'd got him. *(To SHOLTO)* So... I should give the information to the Governor-General, then?

SHOLTO   Well, well, now, don't do anything rash. Let me hear all about it.

SHOLTO holds position as if listening intently as SMALL tells his tale.

SMALL   *(To audience)* I told him the story, with a few small changes so he couldn't identify the places. At last he said:

SHOLTO   This is a very important matter. Say nothing to anyone, and I'll see you soon.

SHOLTO moves upstage.

SMALL   *(To audience)* You're with me now, aren't you? He comes back two nights later, this time with Morstan. Says:

SHOLTO   On reflection, this is probably more of a private matter than anything to trouble government with. If we can agree to terms –

SMALL   The terms are these. Help me to my freedom, and help my three companions to theirs. For that you get a fifth share to divide between you and the captain there.

SHOLTO   A fifth share? Not very tempting.

SMALL   Comes to fifty thousand apiece. For that you bring over a yacht or yawl from Calcutta, stow us on it by night and drop us on the Indian coast.

SHOLTO   What you ask... one of you, maybe...

SMALL   None or all. I've spoken with the other members of the four; it's the only way this works. You get us free; we get the box and cut you in.

SHOLTO   Impossible.

SMALL   Take it or leave it; try winning your Commission back at the card-table.

A beat.

SHOLTO   Confident little cuss, aren't you?

SMALL   I've got half a million reasons to be.

SHOLTO smiles.

SHOLTO   Tell me where the box is hidden. I'll get leave of absence and go back to India in the monthly relief-boat.

SMALL   I'll need to discuss it with the four.

SHOLTO   Discuss it with the...? I've never heard the like. What have three black fellows got to do with our agreement?

SMALL   Everything. Their colour's irrelevant. They're my brothers.

A beat.

SHOLTO   Fine. Talk it through. Find me when you have your answer.

SHOLTO exits.

SMALL   *(To audience)* Course, I knew what they'd say already. Both Singh and Khan had struggled in captivity from the first and were itching to

142

be out. Akbar was his usual calm self, but at last concurred. We would go along with the Major's plan. And, of course... promises are like pie-crusts, as the saying goes. Easily broken. Sholto double-crossed us, he double-crossed Morstan... we'd drawn him maps. Taken him to our treasure. Ours!

A beat.

A few weeks after we knew – really knew – he wasn't coming back, Mahomet Singh and Abdullah Khan were shot trying to commandeer a supply boat.

A beat.

Four years went by. I was allowed some help in the infirmary, so I recruited Dost Akbar. On reflection, that might have been a better way to live out my days, but a terrible vengeance had grown like a virus within me. I had to get off this island. I had to look Sholto in the eye one last time.

A beat.

It so happens that I'm given further medical tasks, and one of them is to re-set the broken leg of one of the indigenous people. Dr. Somerton thinks it's not worth the bother, but I see something in this poor creature's eyes; hear it in his whimpering cry... I re-set the leg. Total success. So much so that this little fellow – Tonga, his name was – starts following me round, sleeping outside my hut; bringing me food.

AKBAR enters.

143

AKBAR   *(In Hindi)* He's like your pet.

SMALL laughs. He is now fluent Hindi.

SMALL   Pets who bring meat give them over; he eats them raw.

AKBAR   You're well-suited then.

SMALL   *(In Hindi)* That's not funny,

AKBAR   It's a little funny.

SMALL   Good English.

AKBAR   Bad English.

AKBAR moves upstage.

SMALL   *(To audience)* It hadn't taken me long to realise that Tonga had a canoe, and I knew he'd be willing to get us off the island... but Akbar wouldn't go.

AKBAR   I won't chase vengeance. Darker emotions feed on the worst parts of our own selves. We need to let those parts go as soon as we can.

SMALL   *(To audience)* He... was such a good man; he...

Sound of shore wash; wind. Lights down low.

The night I decided I had to... to leave; he said he'd cover for us.

AKBAR   Go.

SMALL   *(To audience)* He said.

AKBAR   Exorcise this ghost.

SMALL   I'll come back for you.

A beat. A distant sound of voices and whistles.

AKBAR   No you won't.

SMALL   I will!

AKBAR   I won't be here.

SMALL   Yes; you –

AKBAR   Can you hear the whistles? They're tracking you now. Both of you. I'll stop them. I'll stop the bullets.

SMALL   Dost; please...

AKBAR embraces his friend.

AKBAR   Time to go, Bad English.

SMALL moves downstage and turns.

SMALL   Thank you.

AKBAR smiles and raises his arms. Voices offstage yelling at him to move. He walks smiling into the wings. Lights lower still. There is a volley of gunfire; a flash from the wings.

        (Whispered) Thank you.

Music. As SMALL sits, contemplating his friend's death, the set is once more reconfigured around him. We are back at Baker Street. HOLMES and WATSON have entered and stand by a chair. Lights.

        The time spent once I was back... was, yes, largely as you described it to me in the carriage over here. Tonga... was a loyal friend, but untameable. I would never have killed Bartholomew Sholto; I hope you realise that. I hope his brother can forgive me. Miss Morstan too.

WATSON   Miss Morstan? Why...?

SMALL   Because my hatred... my rage, at the end... I couldn't have any of his heirs getting even the tiniest portion of the treasure. And that, I suppose, has denied her too.

HOLMES   That's what you were dumping over the side of the *Aurora*. Correct?

SMALL   It is.

A beat.

Is there anything else you wish to ask me?

HOLMES   Your inside man at Pondicherry Lodge... Lal Rao, yes?

SMALL   *(Nodding)* He didn't want to help at first...

HOLMES   Who bore a marked resemblance to Dost Akbar.

A beat.

SMALL   You're just guessing now.

WATSON   He never guesses.

HOLMES   As soon as you revealed yourself to be a sentimental man... naturally you offered him your friend's full share.

SMALL   You're too clever by half. Do you know that?

HOLMES merely smiles. ATHELNEY-JONES enters.

ATHELNEY-J.   Well, Mr. Holmes sir, you are a man to be humoured...

HOLMES   As are you, Inspector.

ATHELNEY-J.   Ah; yes... but duty is duty, and I'll feel more at ease when we have our story-teller here safe under lock and key. Of course you'll be wanted at the trial.

HOLMES   Where I shall be sure to testify that Mr. Small did not kill Bartholomew Sholto.

SMALL   Much obliged.

HOLMES   Facts are facts.

ATHELNEY-JONES moves to SMALL.

Enjoy the limelight, Inspector.

ATHELNEY-J.   Oh; well...

HOLMES   No, no. This one is your case, first to last.

At this, ATHELNEY-JONES puffs up with pride.

ATHELNEY-J.   Good-night to you. And to you... Watson.

WATSON smiles. ATHELNEY-JONES exits with SMALL.

HOLMES   Well. A satisfying end to a most perplexing mystery.

WATSON   I'd better head over to Camberwell; inform Miss Morstan.

HOLMES   Yes... an unfortunate turn of events. And yet, something tells me she won't be too downhearted.

WATSON   Holmes, she's just lost a quarter of a million pounds!

HOLMES   But gained something infinitely more precious.

WATSON looks perplexed.

         What? You don't think I don't know you're going to ask for her hand.

WATSON   Is that observation or deduction?

HOLMES   *(Smiling)* A little of both. I really cannot congratulate you.

WATSON   Do you not approve of the match?

HOLMES   On the contrary; she is one of the most charming young ladies I ever met. But love is an emotional thing, and emotions forever interfere with the cold reason which I place above all things. I should never marry myself, lest I bias my judgment.

HOLMES rolls his shoulders; closes his eyes.

         Ah; I feel the wave washing over me.

WATSON   Will you rest?

HOLMES   I don't think I'll have much choice.

WATSON   TI have to say, Holmes, the division seems rather unfair. You've done all the work in this business. I meet the woman I wish to spend my life with; Jones gets the credit... what remains for you?

HOLMES   For me? The needle.

HOLMES reaches for his box and prepares his needle. Music starts to play. WATSON turns to the audience. MARY enters and stands with him.

WATSON   *(To audience)* When we look back at that time, Mary and I marvel at how significant a part coincidence can play in our lives. She did indeed accept my proposal, and has proven every bit the companion I knew she would be. I hope I have provided the same for her.

HOLMES injects. He closes his eyes and puts the needle down.

As to my other companion, Mary would always say this:

MARY   He may keep you at your wits' end, have you out all night on extraordinary adventures risking life and limb, but that is a part of you. When I married you, I married that too, in all of its wonderful madness. And he may not admit it – you may never hear the words come out of his mouth – but trust me, John; he needs you just as much as you need him.

HOLMES holds his violin. He plays a simple, repeated refrain which forms part of the music.

WATSON   *(To audience)* I've still yet to hear him say it. And I've still yet to tell him about the spotted dog, too. Perhaps I will, one day. Or perhaps, like fixing my watch, it will be another thing I never quite get around to doing, as I'm whipped up into another game, marvelling at the skill, the brilliance, of my friend. Mr. Sherlock Holmes.

The musical piece ends as the lights fade to black, then a recorded reprise takes over as the actors take their calls. **The End**